HAL•LEONARD
ESSENTIAL SONGS

Hymns

PIANO VOCAL GUITAR

ISBN 978-1-4234-7397-8

HAL•LEONARD®
CORPORATION

7777 W. BLUEMOUND RD. P.O. BOX 13819 MILWAUKEE, WI 53213

In Australia Contact:
Hal Leonard Australia Pty. Ltd.
4 Lentara Court
Cheltenham, Victoria, 3192 Australia
Email: ausadmin@halleonard.com.au

Visit Hal Leonard Online at
www.halleonard.com

CONTENTS

ABIDE WITH ME

Words by HENRY F. LYTE
Music by WILLIAM H. MONK

Moderately Slow

A - bide with me. Fast falls the e - ven - tide.
I need Thy pre - sence ev - 'ry pass - ing hour.

The dark - ness deep - ens, Lord, with me a - bide.
What but thy grace can foil the tempt - er's pow'r?

When oth - er help - ers fail and com - forts flee, Help of the
Who, like Thy - self, my guide and stay can be? Through cloud and

ALL GLORY, LAUD AND HONOR

Words by THEODULPH OF ORLEANS
Translated by JOHN MASON NEALE
Music by MELCHIOR TESCHNER

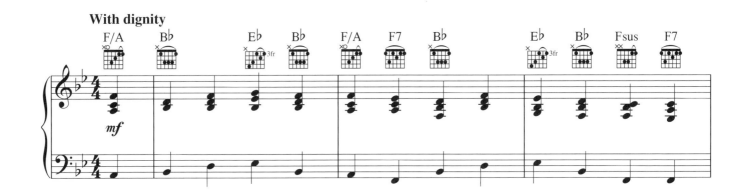

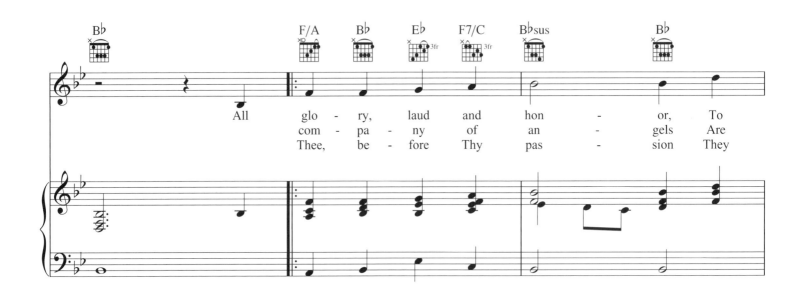

All glo - ry, laud and hon - or, To
com - pa - ny of an - gels Are
Thee, be - fore Thy pas - sion They

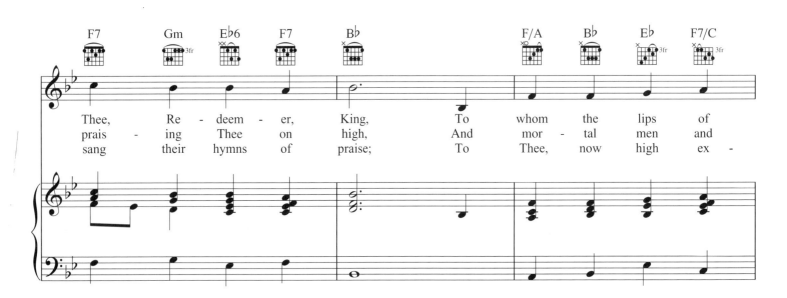

Thee, Re - deem - er, King, To whom the lips of
prais - ing Thee on high, And mor - tal men and
sang their hymns of praise; To Thee, now high ex -

ALL HAIL THE POWER OF JESUS' NAME

Words by EDWARD PERRONET
Music by OLIVER HOLDEN

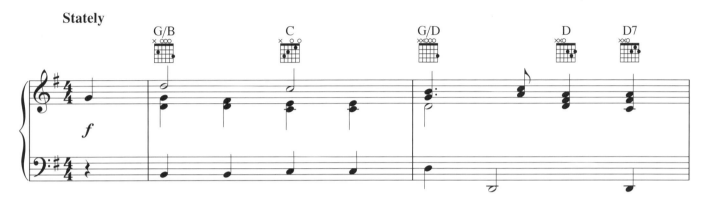

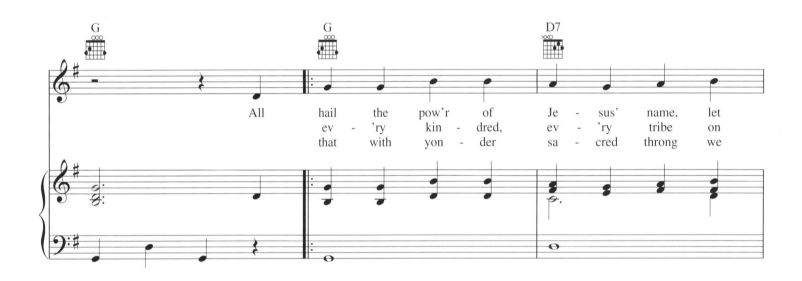

All hail the pow'r of Je - sus' name, let
ev - 'ry kin - dred, ev - 'ry tribe on
that with yon - der sa - cred throng we

an - gels pros - trate fall. Bring forth the roy - al
this ter - res - trial ball to Him all maj - es -
at His feet may fall. We'll join the ev - er -

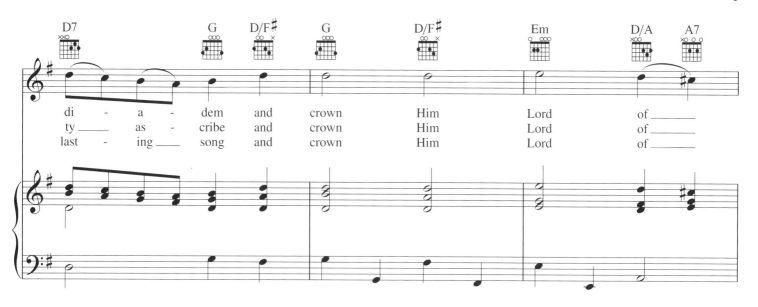

ALL MY TRIALS

African-American Spiritual

ALL THINGS BRIGHT AND BEAUTIFUL

Words by CECIL FRANCES ALEXANDER
17th Century English Melody

AMAZING GRACE

Words by JOHN NEWTON
Traditional American Melody

CLEANSE ME

Words by J. EDWIN ORR
Traditional Maori Melody

Cleanse me from ev-'ry sin and set me free. plead.

2. I praise Thee, Lord, for cleansing me of sin.
   Fulfill Thy Word and make me pure within.
   Fill me with fire where once I burned with shame.
   Grant my desire to magnify Thy Name.

3. Lord, take my life and make it wholly Thine.
   Fill my poor heart with Thy great love divine.
   Take all my will, my passion, self, and pride.
   I now surrender, Lord, in me abide.

4. O Holy Ghost, revival comes from Thee.
   Send a revival, start the work in me.
   Thy Word declares Thou wilt supply our need.
   For blessing now, O Lord, I humbly plead.

AMERICA, THE BEAUTIFUL

Words by KATHERINE LEE BATES
Music by SAMUEL A. WARD

Additional Verses

3. O beautiful for heroes proved
   In liberating strife,
   Who more than self their country loved
   And mercy more than life!
   America! America!
   May God thy gold refine
   'Til all success be nobleness
   And every gain divine.

4. O beautiful for patriot dream
   That sees beyond the years;
   Thine alabaster cities gleam
   Undimmed by human tears.
   America! America!
   God shed His grace on thee,
   And crown thy good with brotherhood,
   From sea to shining sea.

ARE YOU WASHED IN THE BLOOD?

Words and Music by
ELISHA A. HOFFMAN

1. Have you been to Je-sus for the cleans-ing pow'r? Are you
2.-4. *(See additional verses)*

washed in the blood of the Lamb? Are you full-y trust-ing in His

grace this hour? Are you washed in the blood of the Lamb? Are you

Additional Verses

2. Are you walking daily by the Savior's side?
   Are you washed in the blood of the Lamb?
   Do you rest each moment in the Crucified?
   Are you washed in the blood of the Lamb?
   Refrain

3. When the Bridegroom cometh will your robes be white?
   Are you washed in the blood of the Lamb?
   Will your soul be ready for the mansions bright,
   And be washed in the blood of the Lamb?
   Refrain

4. Lay aside the garments that are stained with sin,
   And be washed in the blood of the Lamb;
   There's a fountain flowing for the soul unclean,
   O be washed in the blood of the Lamb!
   Refrain

AT CALVARY

Words by WILLIAM R. NEWELL
Music by DANIEL B. TOWNER

1. Years I spent in van - i - ty and pride,
2.-4. *(See additional verses)*

Car - ing not my Lord was cru - ci - fied, Know - ing not it was for

me He died On Cal - va - ry.

Additional Verses

2. By God's Word at last my sin I learned;
    Then I trembled at the law I'd spurned,
    Till my guilty soul imploring turned To Calvary.
    Refrain

3. Now I've giv'n to Jesus ev'rything,
    Now I gladly own Him as my King,
    Now my raptured soul can only sing Of Calvary.
    Refrain

4. Oh, the love that drew salvation's plan!
    Oh, the grace that bro't it down to man!
    Oh, the mighty gulf that God did span At Calvary.
    Refrain

AT THE CROSS

Words by ISAAC WATTS and RALPH E. HUDSON
Music by RALPH E. HUDSON

1. A -

las! and did my Sav - ior bleed? And did my Sov - reign
2. it for crimes that I have done He groaned up - on the
3. might the sun in dark - ness hole He And shut His glo - ries
4. drops of grief can ne'er re - pay the debt of love I

die? Would He de - vote that sa - cred head For
tree? A - maz - ing pit - y! grace un - known! And
in, When Christ, the might - y Mak - er, died For
owe: Here, Lord, I give my - self a - way— 'Tis

BATTLE HYMN OF THE REPUBLIC

Words by JULIA WARD HOWE
Music by WILLIAM STEFFE

1. Mine eyes have seen the glo - ry of the com - ing of the Lord. He is
2. seen him in the watch - fires of the hun - dred cir - cling camps. They have
3.-5. *(See additional verses)*

tram - pling out the vin - tage where the grapes of wrath are stored. He hath
build - ed Him an al - tar in the eve - ning dews and damps. I have

loos'd the fate - ful light - ning of His ter - ri - ble swift sword. His
read His right - eous sen - tence by the dim and flar - ing lamps. His

Additional Verses

3. I have read a fiery gospel writ in burnished rows of steel.
   As ye deal with my contempters, so with you my grace shall deal.
   Let the hero born of woman crush the serpent with his heel,
   Since God is marching on.

4. He has sounded forth the trumpet that shall never call retreat.
   He is sifting out the hearts of men before His judgement seat.
   O be swift, my soul, to answer Him, be jubilant, my feet.
   Our God is marching on.

5. In the beauty of the lilies, Christ was born across the sea
   With a glory in His bosom that transfigures you and me.
   As He died to make men holy, let us die to make men free,
   While God is marching on.

BEAUTIFUL ISLE OF SOMEWHERE

Words by JESSIE B. POUNDS
Music by JOHN S. FEARIS

Moderately

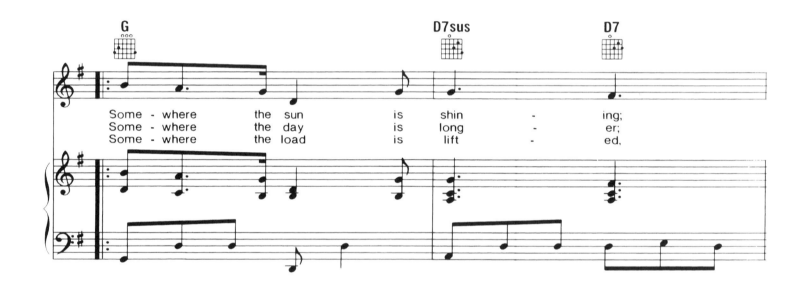

G   D7sus   D7

Some - where   the sun   is   shin   -   ing;
Some - where   the day   is   long   -   er;
Some - where   the load   is   lift   -   ed,

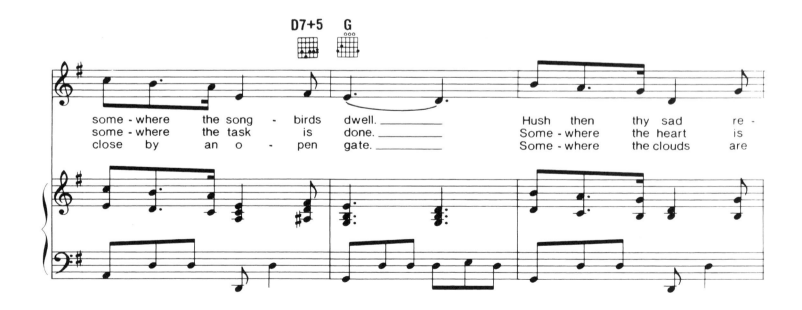

D7+5   G

some - where   the song - birds   dwell. _____
some - where   the task   is   done. _____
close   by   an o - pen   gate. _____

Hush then   thy sad   re -
Some - where   the heart   is
Some - where   the clouds   are

BEAUTIFUL SAVIOR

Words from *Munsterisch Gesangbuch*
Translated by JOSEPH A. SEISS
Music adapted from a Silesian Folk Tune

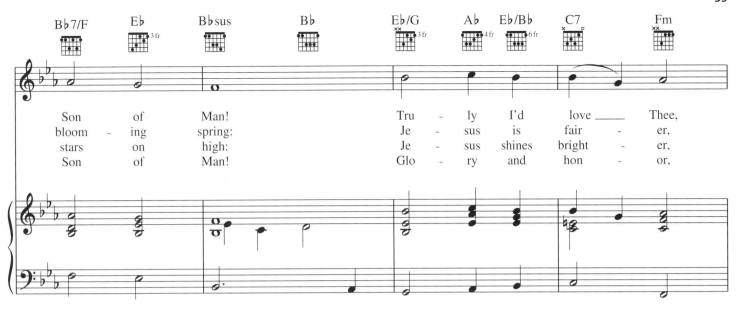

Son of Man! Tru - ly I'd love ____ Thee,
bloom - ing spring: Je - sus is fair - er,
stars on high: Je - sus shines bright - er,
Son of Man! Glo - ry and hon - or,

Tru - ly I'd serve ____ Thee, Light of my
Je - sus is pur - er; He makes our
Je - sus shines pur - er Than all the
Praise, ad - o - ra - tion, Now and for -

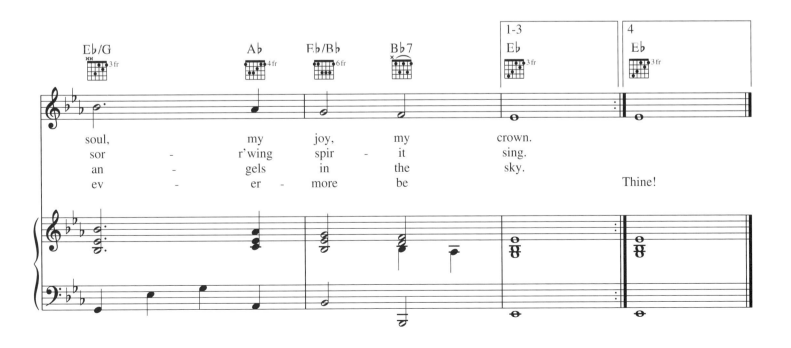

soul, my joy, my crown.
sor - r'wing spir - it sing.
an - gels in the sky.
ev - er - more be Thine!

BLESSED BE THE NAME

Words by WILLIAM H. CLARK (verses)
and RALPH E. HUDSON (refrain)
Traditional Music

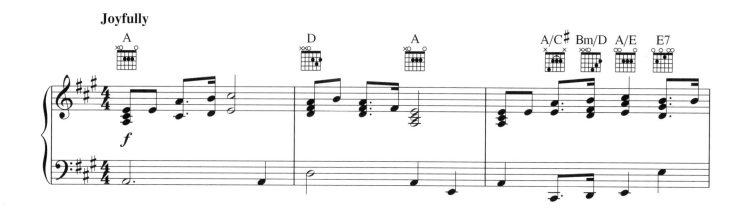

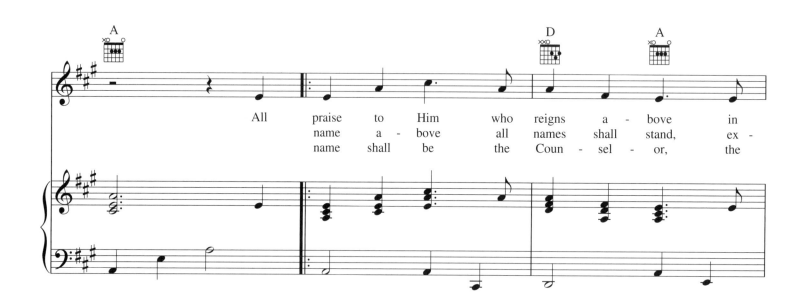

All praise to Him who reigns a - bove in
name a - bove all names shall stand, ex -
name shall be the Coun - sel - or, the

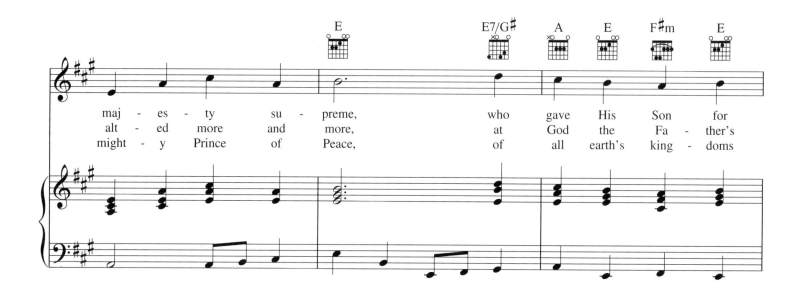

maj - es - ty su - preme, who gave His Son for
alt - ed more and more, at God the Fa - ther's
might - y Prince of Peace, of all earth's king - doms

BLEST BE THE TIE THAT BINDS

Words by JOHN FAWCETT
Music by JOHANN G. NÄGELI

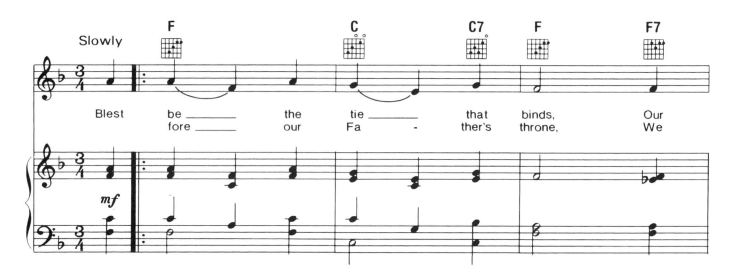

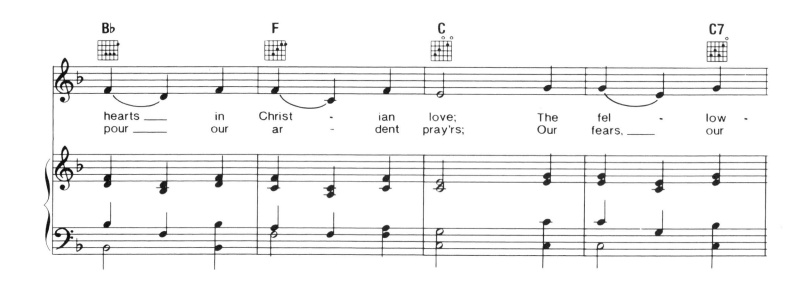

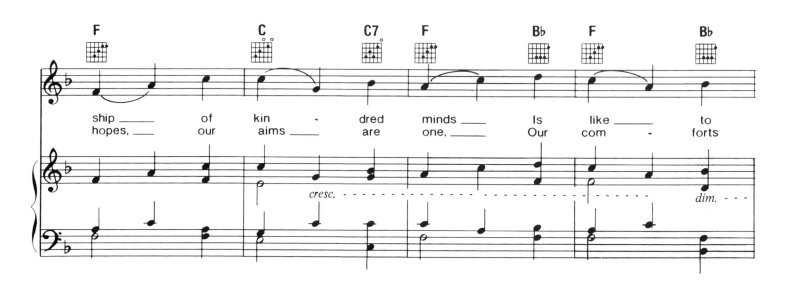

BREAK THOU THE BREAD OF LIFE

Words by MARY ARTEMESIA LATHBURY
Music by WILLIAM FISKE SHERWIN

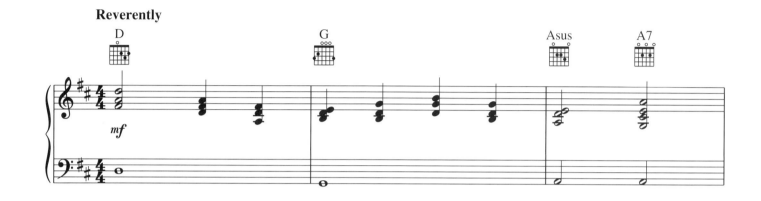

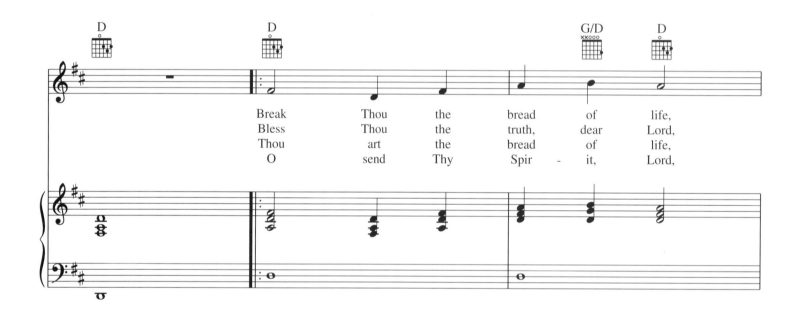

Break Thou the bread of life,
Bless Thou the truth, dear Lord,
Thou art the bread of life,
O send Thy Spir - it, Lord,

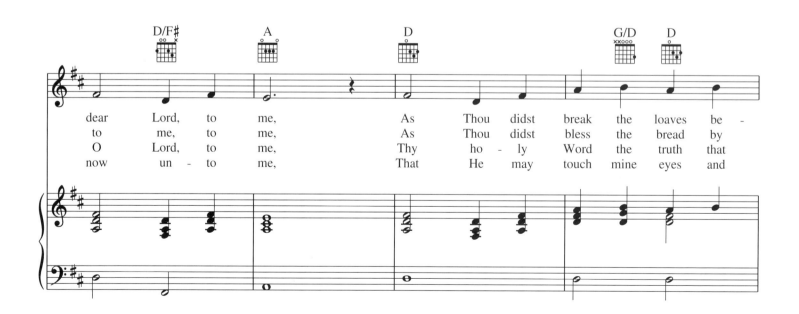

dear Lord, to me, As Thou didst break the loaves be -
to me, to me, As Thou didst bless the bread by
O Lord, to me, Thy ho - ly Word the truth that
now un - to me, That He may touch mine eyes and

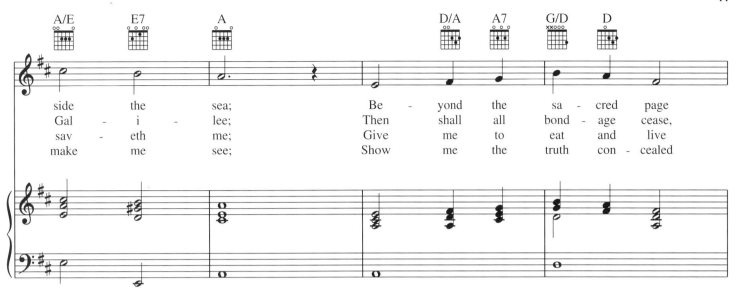

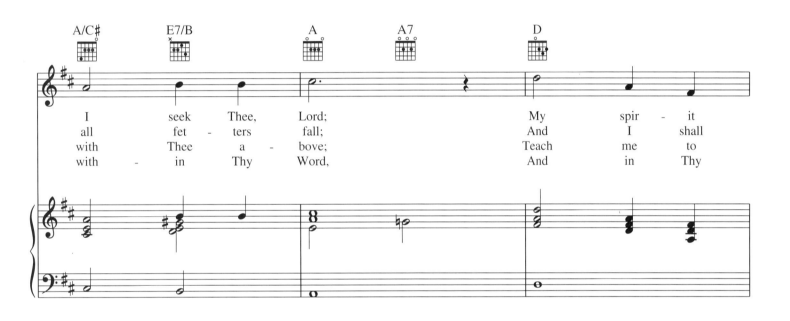

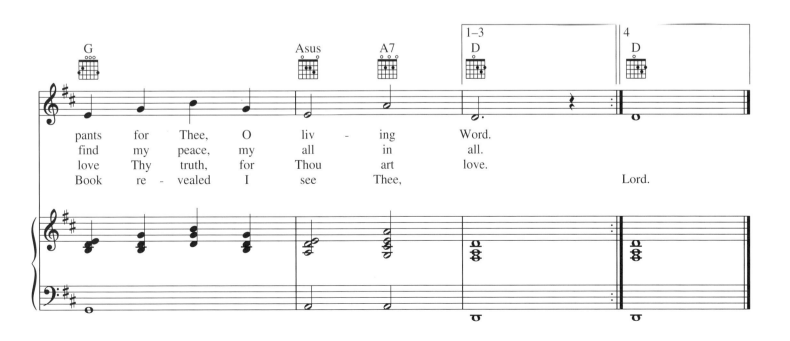

BRIGHTEN THE CORNER
WHERE YOU ARE

Words by INA DULEY OGDON
Music by CHARLES H. GABRIEL

BRINGING IN THE SHEAVES

Words by KNOWLES SHAW
Music by GEORGE A. MINOR

Medium Tempo

Sow - ing in the morn - ing, sow - ing seeds of kind - ness,
Sow - ing in the sun - shine, sow - ing in the shad - ows;

Sow - ing in the noon - tide and the dew - y eve; Wait - ing for the har - vest,
Fear - ing nei - ther clouds nor win - ter's chill - ing breeze; By and by the har - vest

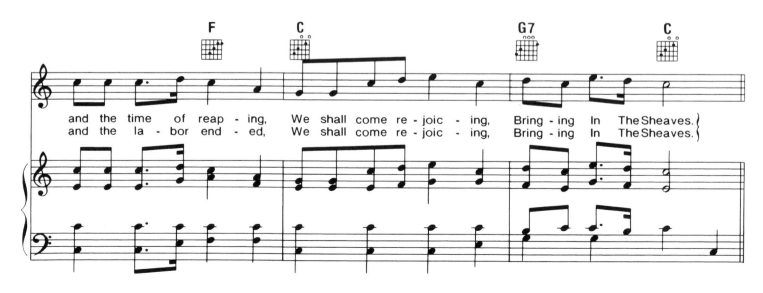

and the time of reap - ing, We shall come re - joic - ing, Bring - ing In The Sheaves.
and the la - bor end - ed, We shall come re - joic - ing, Bring - ing In The Sheaves.

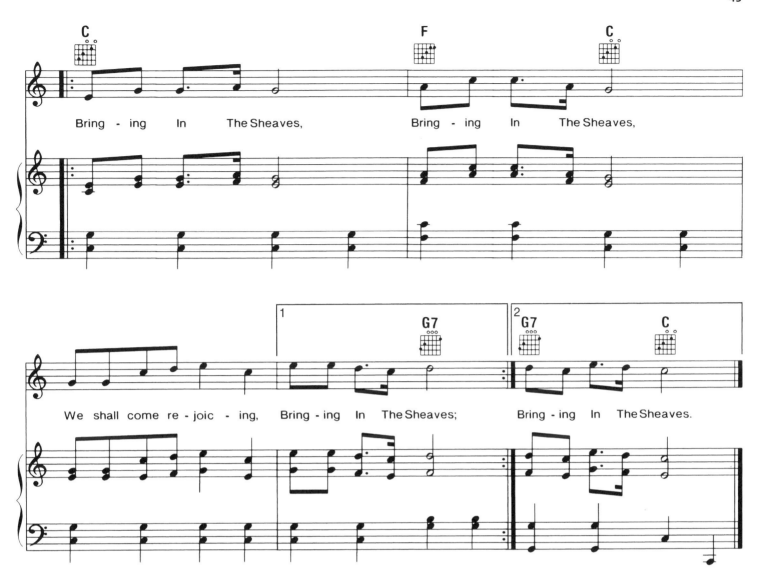

Bring - ing In The Sheaves, Bring - ing In The Sheaves,

We shall come re - joic - ing, Bring - ing In The Sheaves; Bring - ing In The Sheaves.

3. Going forth with weeping, sowing for the Master.
Tho' the loss sustained our spirit often grieves;
When our weeping's over, He will bid us welcome,
We shall come rejoicing, bringing in the sheaves.

CHRIST AROSE
(Low in the Grave He Lay)

Words and Music by
ROBERT LOWRY

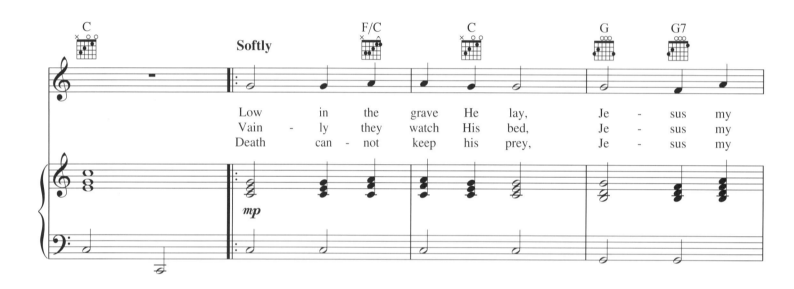

Low in the grave He lay, Je - sus my
Vain - ly they watch His bed, Je - sus my
Death can - not keep his prey, Je - sus my

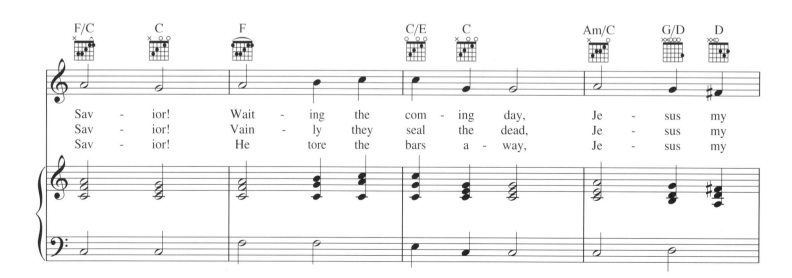

Sav - ior! Wait - ing the com - ing day, Je - sus my
Sav - ior! Vain - ly they seal the dead, Je - sus my
Sav - ior! He tore the bars a - way, Je - sus my

CHRIST THE LORD IS RISEN TODAY

Words by CHARLES WESLEY
Music adapted from *Lyra Davidica*

CHURCH IN THE WILDWOOD

Words and Music by
DR. WILLIAM S. PITTS

THE CHURCH'S ONE FOUNDATION

Words by SAMUEL JOHN STONE
Music by SAMUEL SEBASTIAN WESLEY

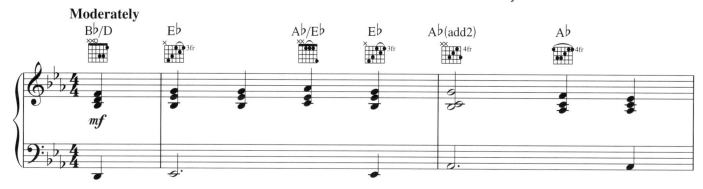

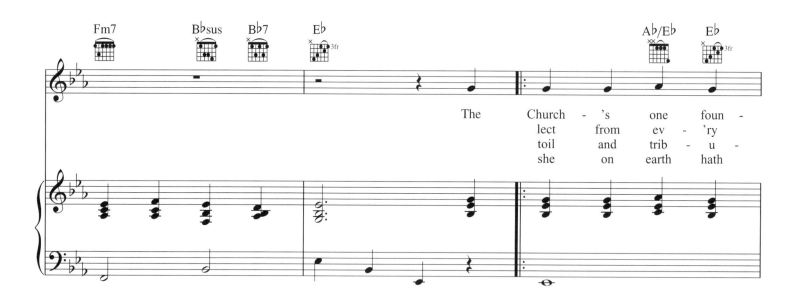

The Church's one foun-
lect from ev-'ry
she on earth hath

da - tion is Je - sus Christ her Lord; She
na - tion, yet one o'er all the earth; Her
la - tion, and tu - mult of her war, She
u - nion with God, the Three in One, And

53

COME, THOU ALMIGHTY KING

Traditional
Music by FELICE GIARDINI

COUNT YOUR BLESSINGS

Words by JOHNSON OATMAN, JR.
Music by EDWIN O. EXCELL

When up-on life's bil-lows you are tem-pest tossed,
Are you ev-er bur-dened with a load of care?
When you look at oth-ers with their lands and gold,
So, a-mid the con-flict, wheth-er great or small,

when you are dis-cour-aged, think-ing all is lost,
Does the cross seem heav-y you are called to bear?
think that Christ has prom-ised you His wealth un-told.
do not be dis-cour-aged; God is o-ver all.

CROWN HIM WITH MANY CROWNS

Words by MATTHEW BRIDGES
and GODFREY THRING
Music by GEORGE JOB ELVEY

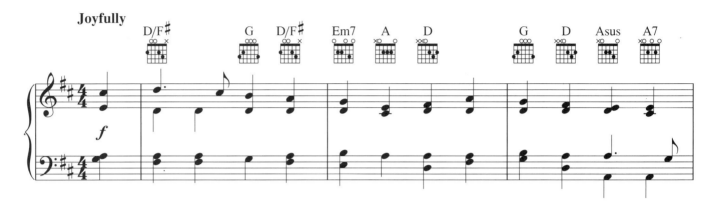

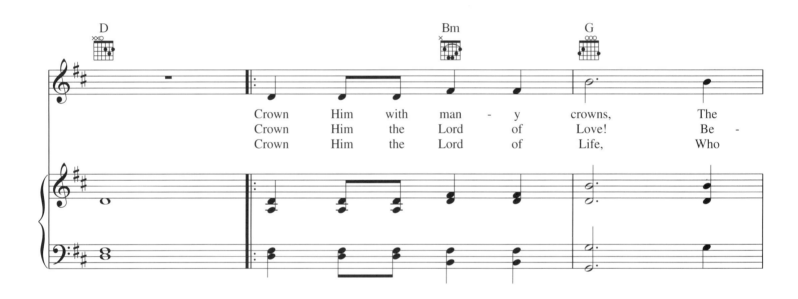

Crown Him with man - y crowns, The
Crown Him the Lord of Love! The Be -
Crown Him the Lord of Life, Who

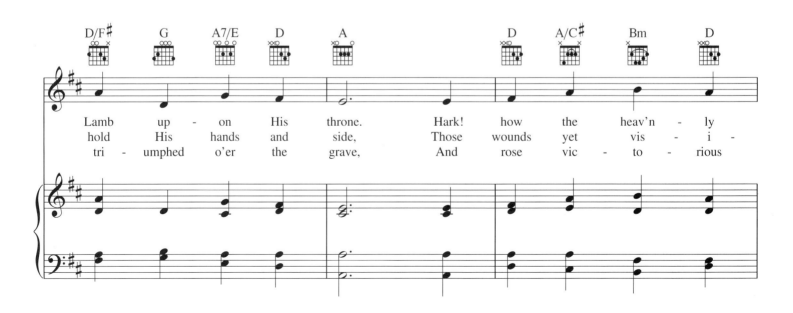

Lamb up - on His throne. Hark! how the heav'n - ly
hold His hands and side, Those wounds yet vis - i -
tri - umphed o'er the grave, And rose vic - to - rious

DEEP RIVER

African-American Spiritual
Based on Joshua 3

DOES JESUS CARE?

Words by FRANK E. GRAEFF
Music by J. LINCOLN HALL

DOWN BY THE RIVERSIDE

African-American Spiritual

HE'S GOT THE WHOLE WORLD
IN HIS HANDS

Traditional Spiritual

EVERY TIME I FEEL THE SPIRIT

African-American Spiritual

FAIREST LORD JESUS

Words from *Münster Gesangbuch*
Verse 4 by JOSEPH A. SEISS
Music from *Schlesische Volkslieder*

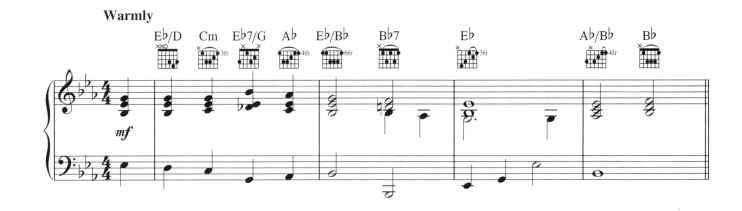

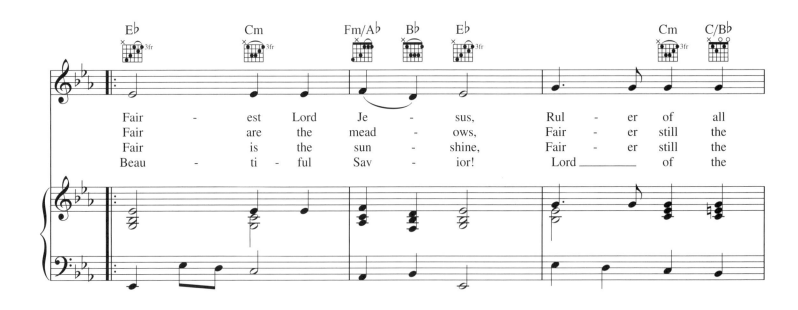

Fair - est Lord Je - sus, Rul - er of all
Fair are the mead - ows, Fair - er still the
Fair is the sun - shine, Fair - er still the
Beau - ti - ful Sav - ior! Lord _____ of the

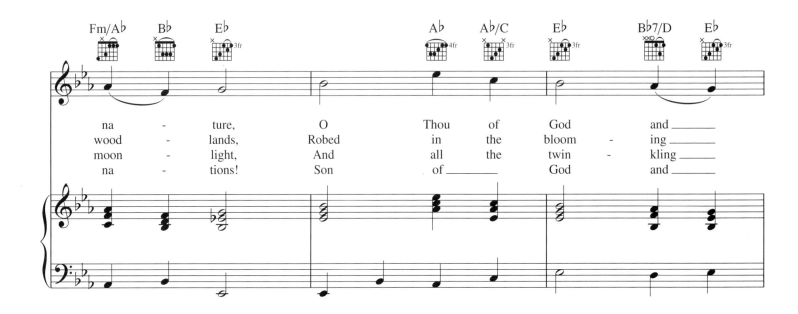

na - ture, O Thou of God and _____
wood - lands, Robed in the bloom - ing _____
moon - light, And all the twin - kling _____
na - tions! Son of _____ God and _____

FAITH OF OUR FATHERS

Words by FREDERICK WILLIAM FABER
Music by HENRI F. HEMY and JAMES G. WALTON

78

FOOTSTEPS OF JESUS

Words by MARY B.C. SLADE
Music by ASA B. EVERETT

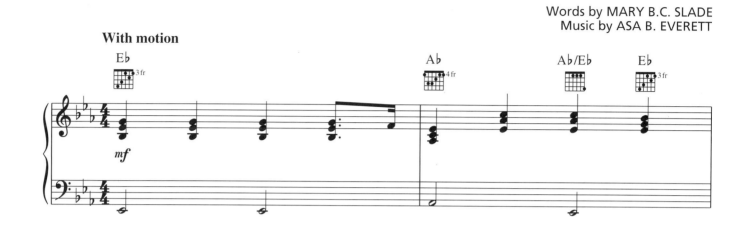

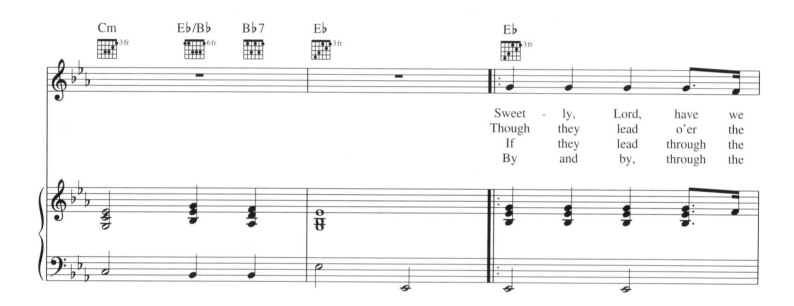

Sweet - ly, Lord, have we
Though they lead o'er the
If they lead through the
By and by, through the

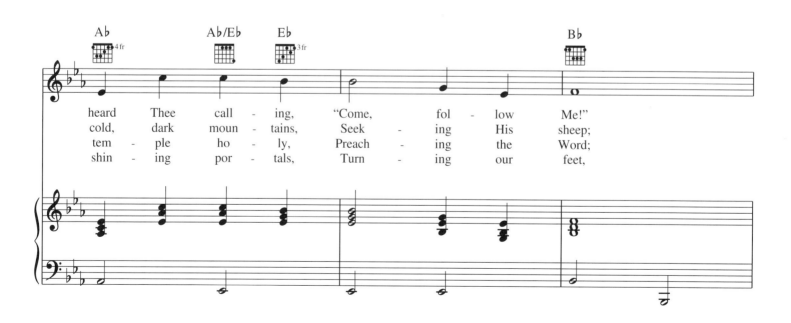

heard Thee call - ing, "Come, fol - low Me!"
cold, dark moun - tains, Seek - ing His sheep;
tem - ple ho - ly, Preach - ing the Word;
shin - ing por - tals, Turn - ing our feet,

FOR ALL THE BLESSINGS
OF THE YEAR

Words by ALBERT H. HUTCHINSON
Music by ROBERT N. QUAILE

FOR THE BEAUTY OF THE EARTH

Words by FOLLIOT S. PIERPOINT
Music by CONRAD KOCHER

Gently, flowing

For the ___ beau - ty of the earth, for the glo - ry of the skies,

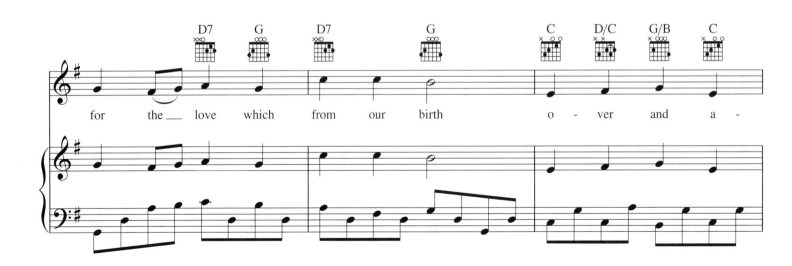

for the ___ love which from our birth o - ver and a -

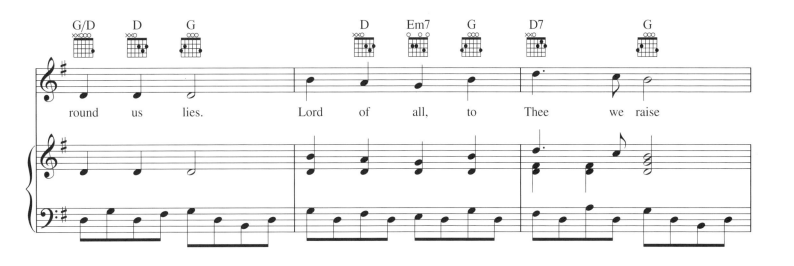

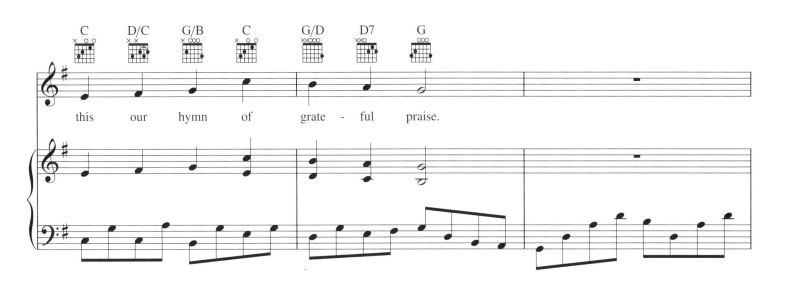

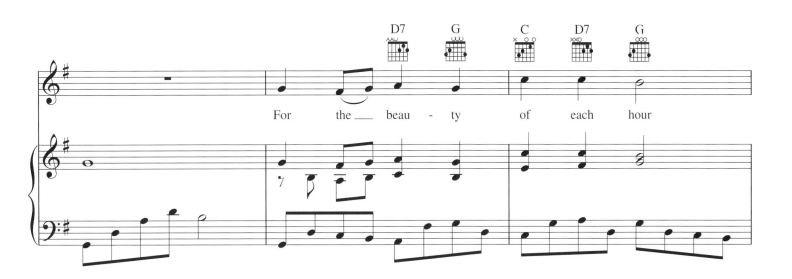

85

GIVE ME THAT OLD TIME RELIGION

Traditional

3. It was good for old Abe Lincoln;
It was good for old Abe Lincoln.
It was good for old Abe Lincoln,
And it's good enough for me.

GOD WILL TAKE CARE OF YOU

Words by CIVILLA D. MARTIN
Music by W. STILLMAN MARTIN

Moderately

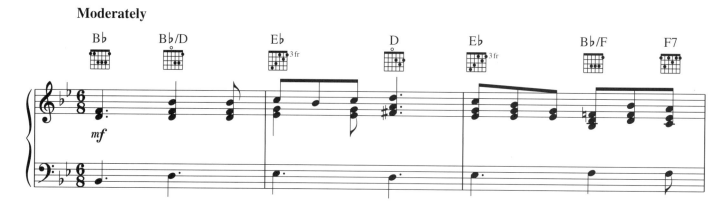

Be not dis - mayed ___ what - e'er be - tide;
Through days of toil ___ when heart doth fail;
All you may need ___ He will pro - vide;
No mat - ter what ___ may be the test,

God will take care of you. ___

Be - neath His wings ___ of
When dan - gers fierce ___ your
Noth - ing you ask ___ will
Lean, wea - ry one, ___ up -

HALLELUJAH, WE SHALL RISE

By J.E. THOMAS

HE HIDETH MY SOUL

Words by FANNY J. CROSBY
Music by WILLIAM J. KIRKPATRICK

HE KEEPS ME SINGING

Words and Music by
LUTHER B. BRIDGERS

HE LEADETH ME

Words by JOSEPH H. GILMORE
Music by WILLIAM B. BRADBURY

HIGHER GROUND

Words by JOHNSON OATMAN, JR.
Music by CHARLES H. GABRIEL

Moderately

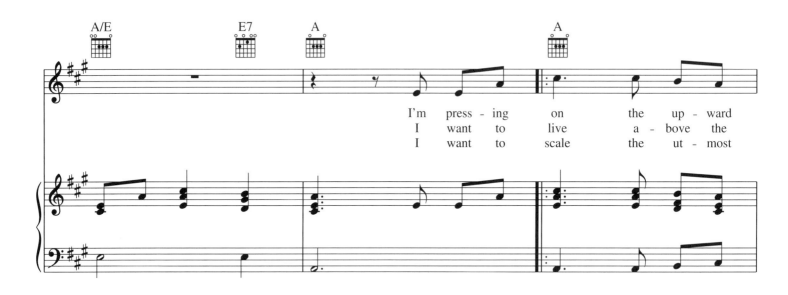

I'm press-ing on the up-ward
I want to live a-bove the
I want to scale the ut-most

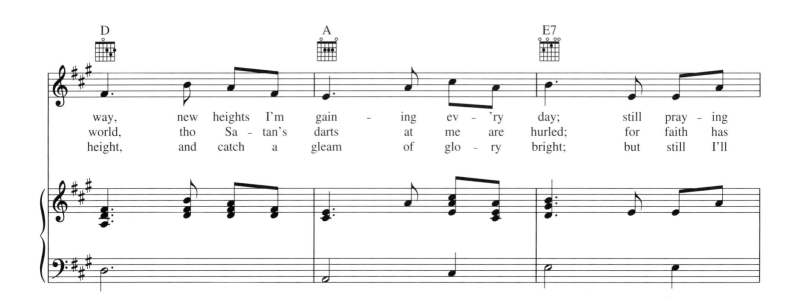

way, new heights I'm gain-ing ev-'ry day; still pray-ing
world, tho Sa-tan's darts at me are hurled; for faith has
height, and catch a gleam of glo-ry bright; but still I'll

99

HIS EYE IS ON THE SPARROW

Words by CIVILLA D. MARTIN
Music by CHARLES H. GABRIEL

HOLY GOD, WE PRAISE THY NAME

Words and Music from *Katholisches Gesangbuch*
Words attributed to IGNAZ FRANZ
Translated by CLARENCE WALWORTH

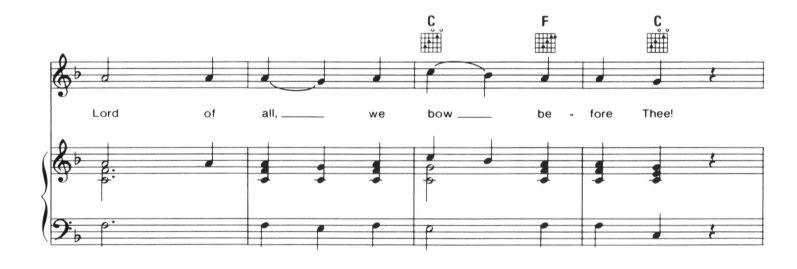

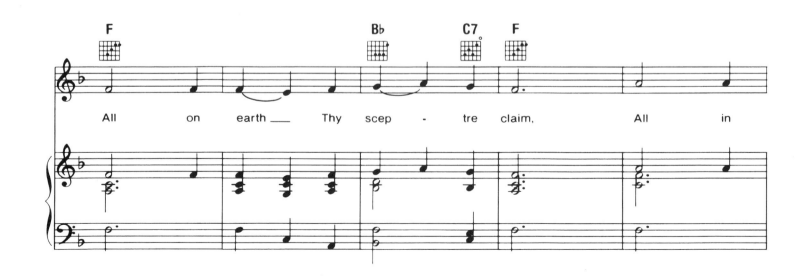

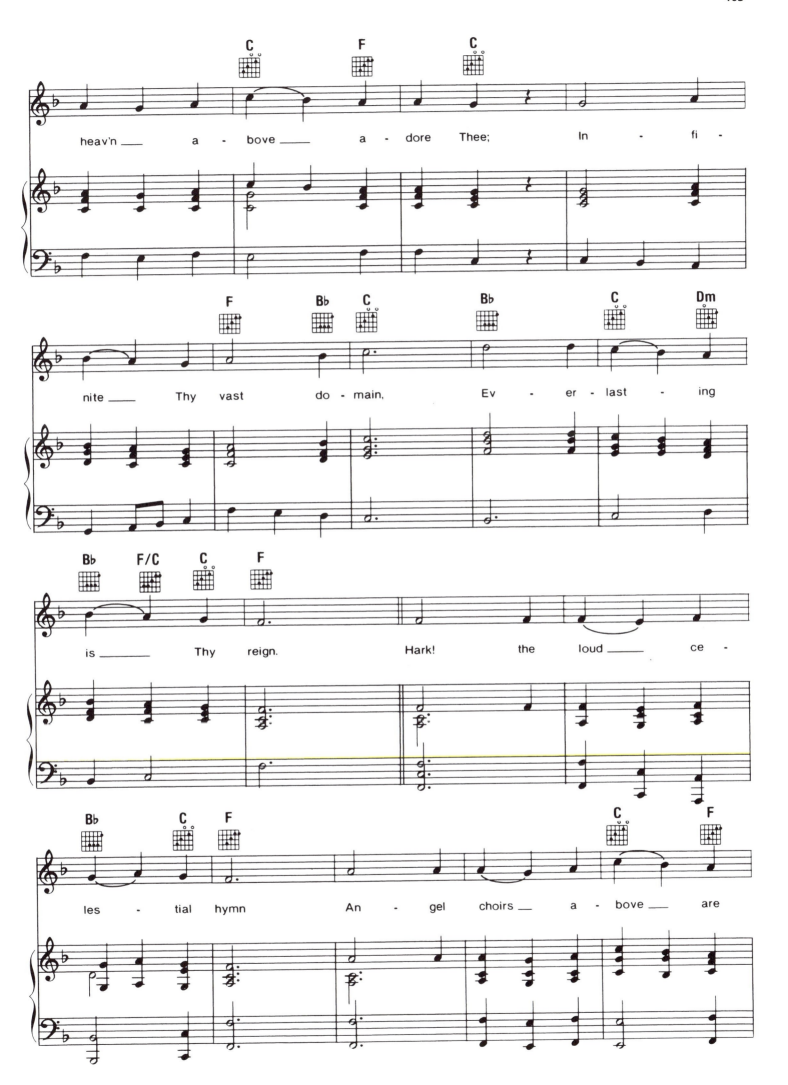

HOLY, HOLY, HOLY

Text by REGINALD HEBER
Music by JOHN B. DYKES

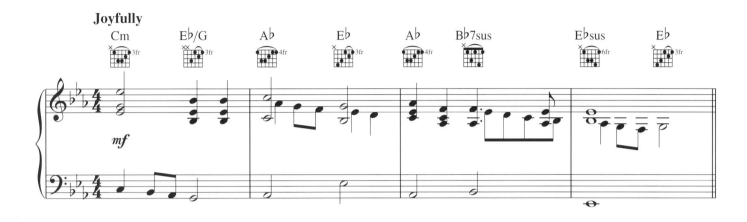

Ho - ly, ho - ly, ho - ly! Lord God Al -
Ho - ly, ho - ly, ho - ly! All the saints a -

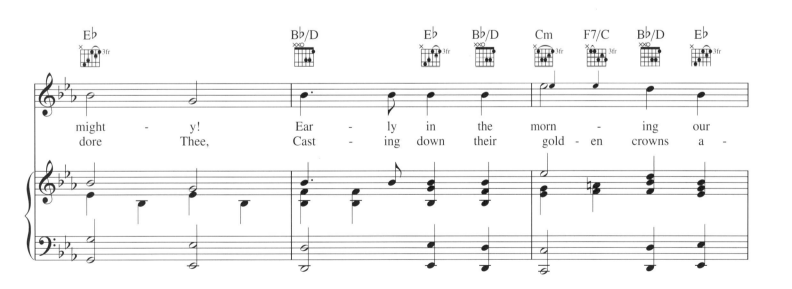

might - y! Ear - ly in the morn - ing our
dore Thee, Cast - ing down their gold - en crowns a -

HOSANNA, LOUD HOSANNA

Words by JENETTE THRELFALL,
Based on Matthew 21:1-11
Music from *Gesangbuch der Herzogl*

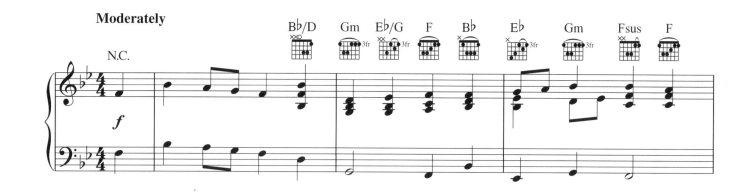

"Ho - san - na, ___ loud ho - san - - - na!" the
Ol - i - vet they fol - lowed 'mid
san - na ___ in the high - est!" That

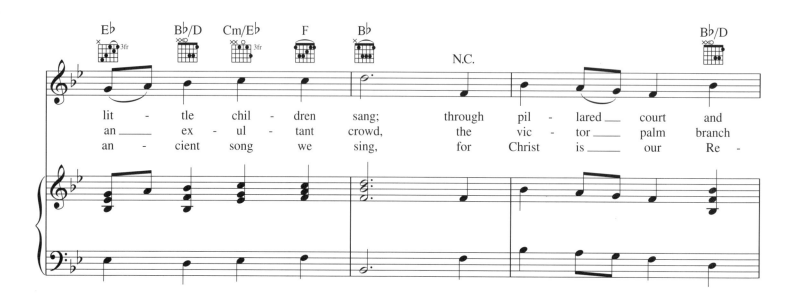

lit - tle chil - dren sang; through pil - lared ___ court and
an ___ ex - ul - tant crowd, the vic - tor ___ palm and branch
an - cient song we sing, for Christ is ___ our Re -

HOW FIRM A FOUNDATION

Words from JOHN RIPPON'S *A Selection of Hymns*
Early American Melody

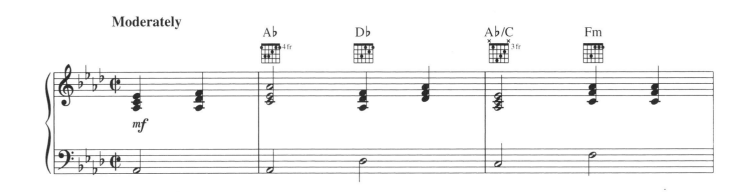

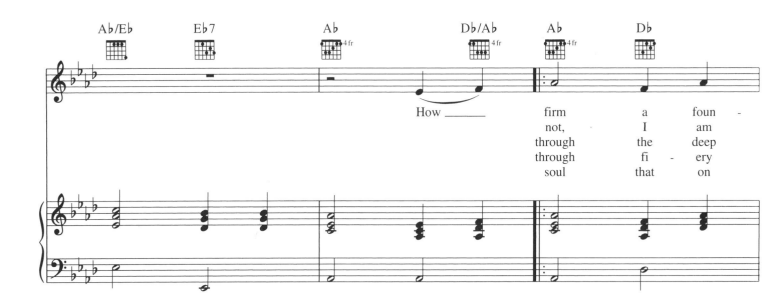

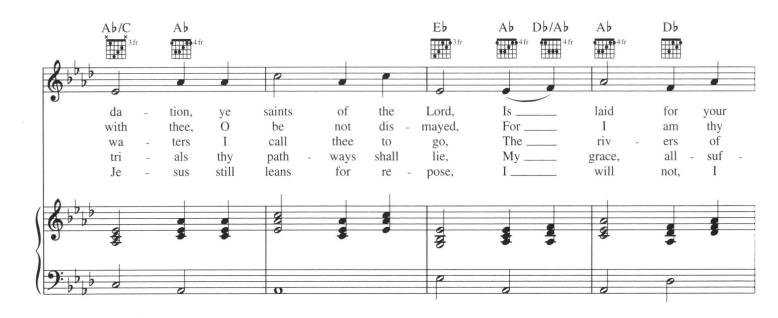

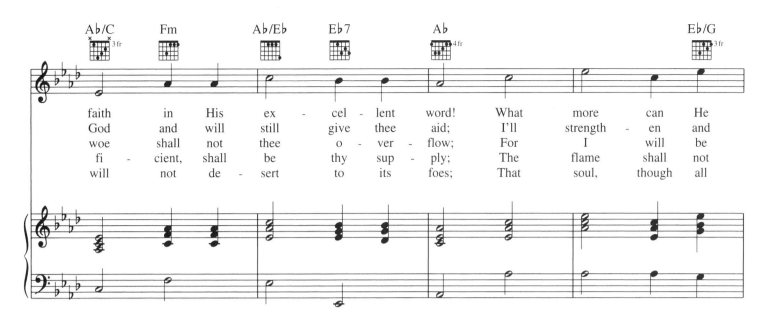

faith in His ex - cel - lent word! What more can He
God and will still give thee aid; I'll strength - en and
woe shall not thee o - ver - flow; For I will be
fi - cient, shall be thy sup - ply; The flame shall not
will not de - sert to its foes; That soul, though all

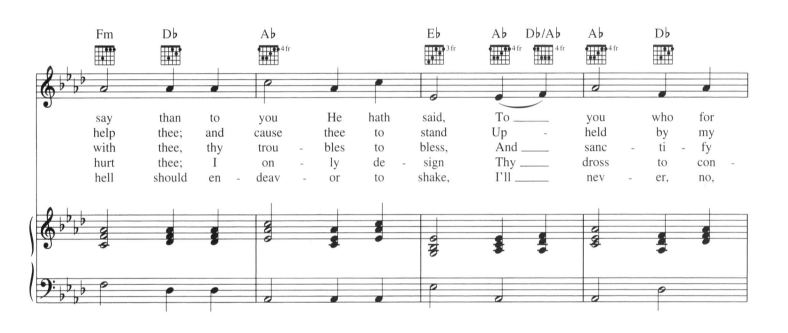

say than to you He hath said, To _____ you who for
help thee; and cause thee to stand Up - held by my
with thee, thy trou - bles to bless, And _____ sanc - ti - fy
hurt thee; I on - ly de - sign Thy _____ dross to con -
hell should en - deav - or to shake, I'll _____ nev - er, no,

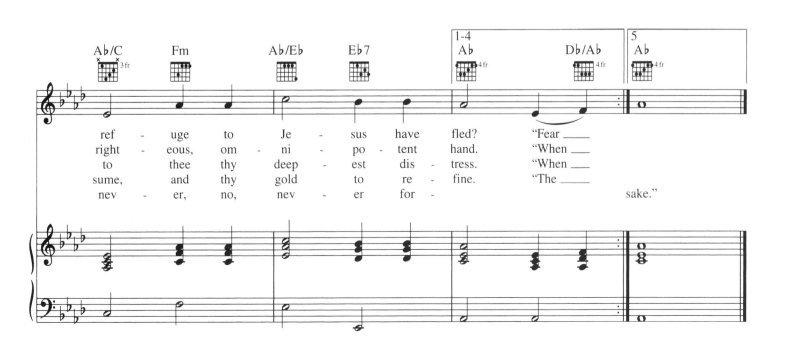

ref - uge to Je - sus have fled? "Fear _____
right - eous, om - ni - po - tent hand. "When _____
to thee thy deep - est dis - tress. "When _____
sume, and thy gold to re - fine. "The _____
nev - er, no, nev - er for - sake."

I HAVE DECIDED TO FOLLOW JESUS

Folk Melody from India
Arranged by AUILA READ

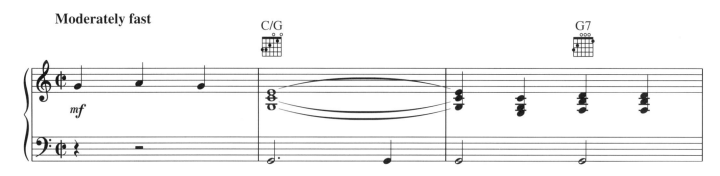

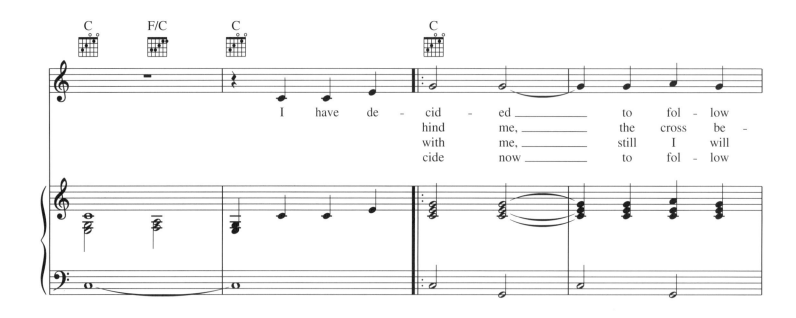

I KNOW THAT MY REDEEMER LIVES

Words by SAMUEL MEDLEY
Music by JOHN HATTON

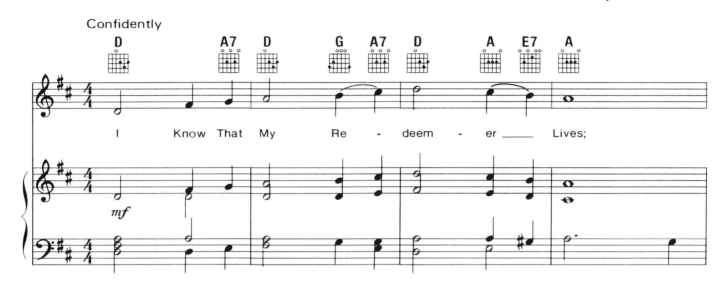

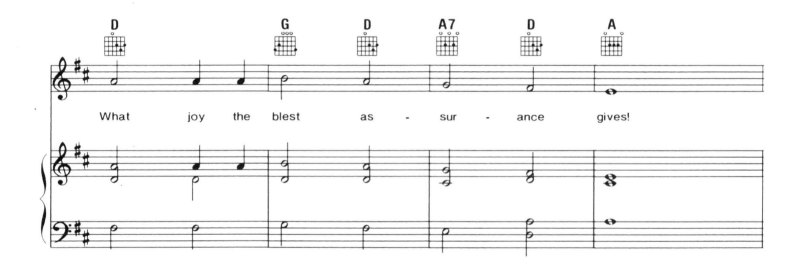

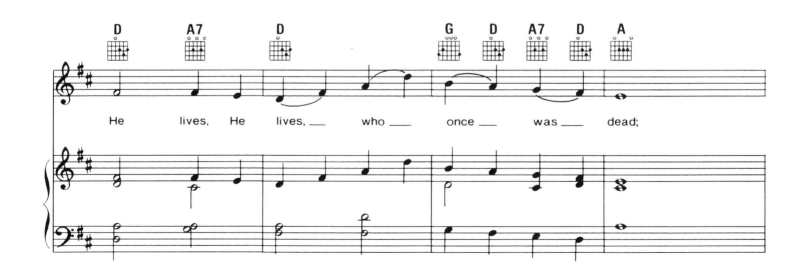

I LOVE TO TELL THE STORY

Words by A. CATHERINE HANKEY
Music by WILLIAM G. FISCHER

117

I SING THE MIGHTY POWER OF GOD

Words by ISAAC WATTS
Music from *Gesangbuch der Herzogl*

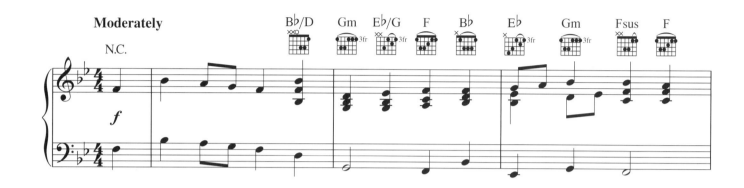

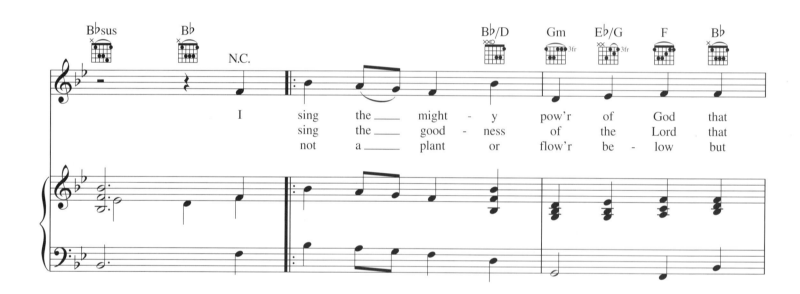

I sing the ___ might - y pow'r of God that
sing the ___ good - ness of the Lord that
not a ___ plant or flow'r be - low but

made ___ the moun - tains rise, that spread the ___ flow - ing
filled ___ the earth with food. He formed the ___ crea - tures
makes ___ Thy glo - ries known. And clouds a - rise and

I'VE GOT PEACE LIKE A RIVER

Traditional

IN THE GARDEN

Words and Music by
C. AUSTIN MILES

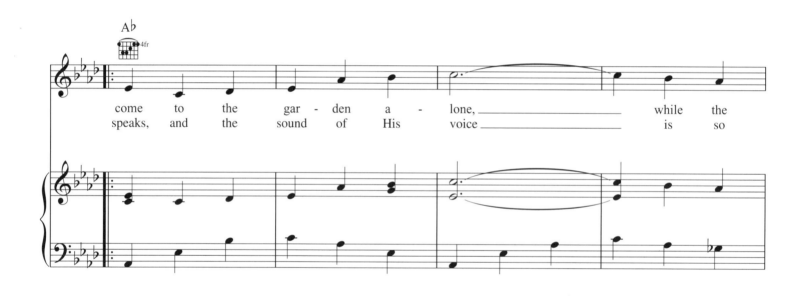

come to the gar - den a - lone, _____ while the
speaks, and the sound of His voice _____ is so

dew is still on the ros - es; and the
sweet the birds hush their sing - ing; and the

voice I hear, fall - ing on my ear, the
mel - o - dy that He gave to me with -

Son of God dis - clos - es. } And He
in my heart is ring - ing.

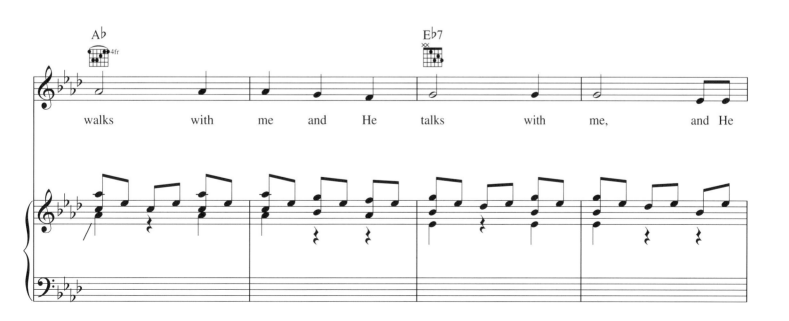

walks with me and He talks with me, and He

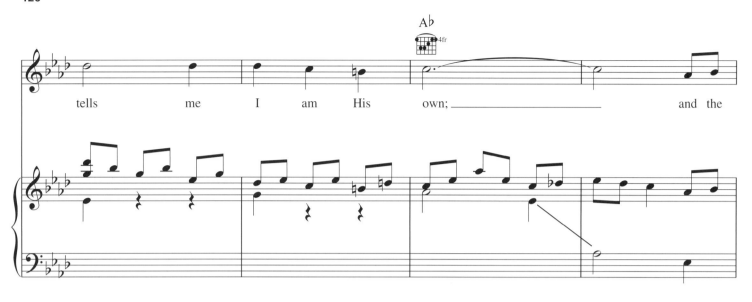

tells me I am His own; _____ and the

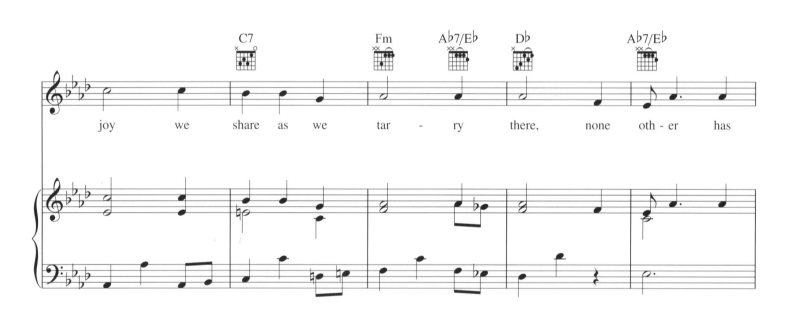

joy we share as we tar - ry there, none oth - er has

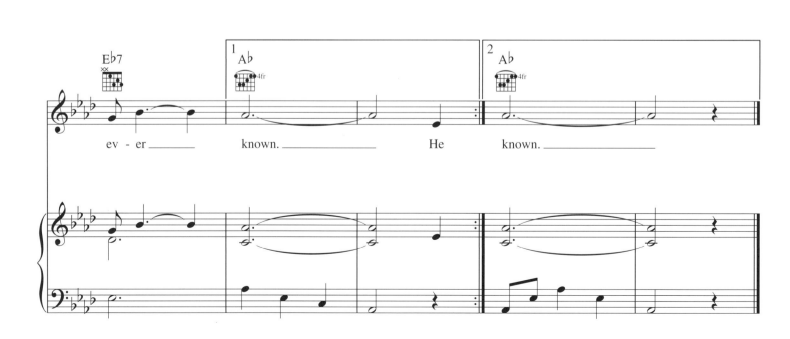

ev - er _____ known. _____ He known. _____

JESUS, THE VERY THOUGHT OF THEE

Words attributed to BERNARD OF CLAIRVAUX
Translated by EDWARD CASWALL
Music by JOHN BACCHUS DYKES

IN THE HOUR OF TRIAL

Words by JAMES MONTGOMERY
Altered by FRANCES A. HUTTON
Music by SPENCER LANE

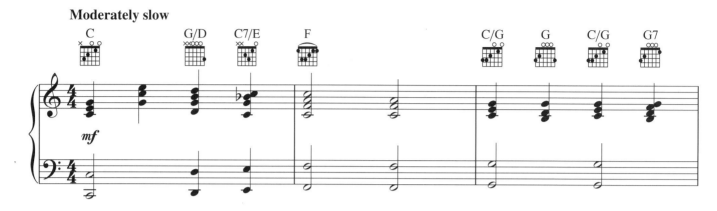

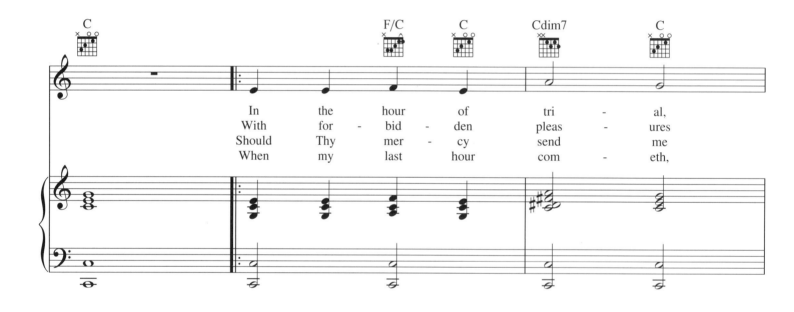

In the hour of tri - al,
With for - bid - den pleas - ures
Should Thy mer - cy send me
When my last hour com - eth,

Je - sus, plead for me, lest by base de -
should this vain world charm, or by its sor - did
sor - row, toil and woe, or should pain at -
fraught with strife and pain, when my dust re -

JESUS, LOVER OF MY SOUL

Words by CHARLES WESLEY
Music by SIMEON B. MARSH

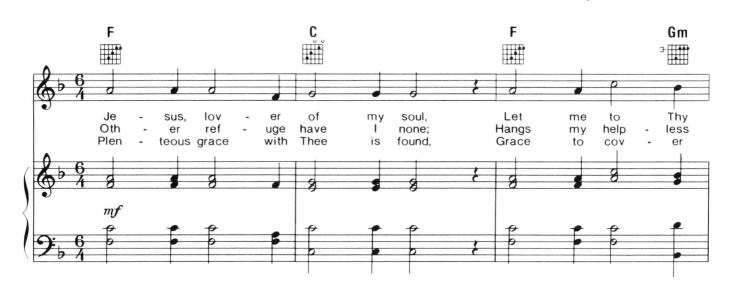

Je - sus, lov - er of my soul, Let me to Thy
Oth - er ref - uge have I none; Hangs my help - less
Plen - teous grace with Thee is found, Grace to cov - er

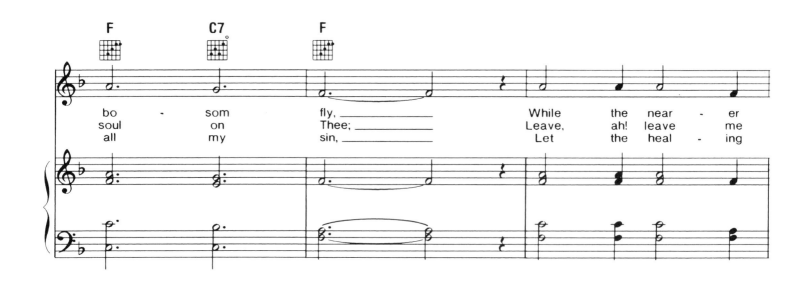

bo - som fly, _____ While the near - er
soul on Thee; _____ Leave, ah! leave me
all my sin, _____ Let the heal - ing

wa - ters roll, While the tem - pest still is
not a - lone, Still sup - port and com - fort
streams a - bound; Make and keep me pure with -

JESUS LOVES ME

Words by ANNA B. WARNER
Music by WILLIAM B. BRADBURY

JESUS, SAVIOR, PILOT ME

Words by EDWARD HOPPER
Music by JOHN E. GOULD

JESUS, THOU JOY OF LOVING HEARTS

Words attributed to BERNARD OF CLAIRVAUX
Translated by RAY PALMER
Music by HENRY BAKER

JUST A CLOSER WALK WITH THEE

Traditional
Arranged by KENNETH MORRIS

JUST AS I AM

Words by CHARLOTTE ELLIOTT
Music by WILLIAM B. BRADBURY

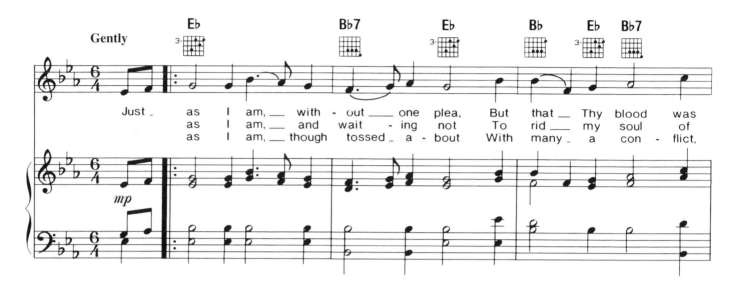

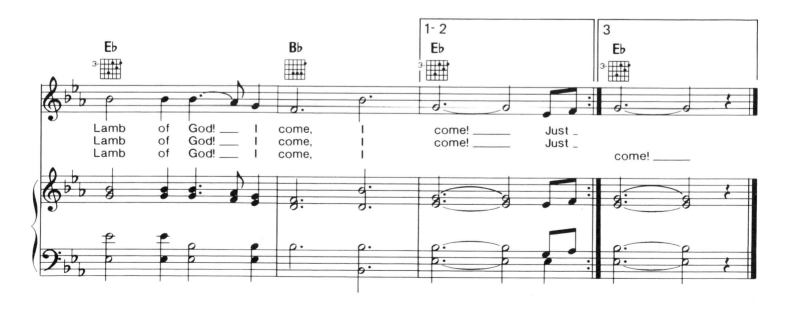

KUM BA YAH

Traditional Spiritual

LET US BREAK BREAD TOGETHER

Traditional Spiritual

THE OLD RUGGED CROSS

Words and Music by
Rev. GEORGE BENNARD

On a hill far a - way stood an old rug - ged
old rug - ged cross I will ev - er be

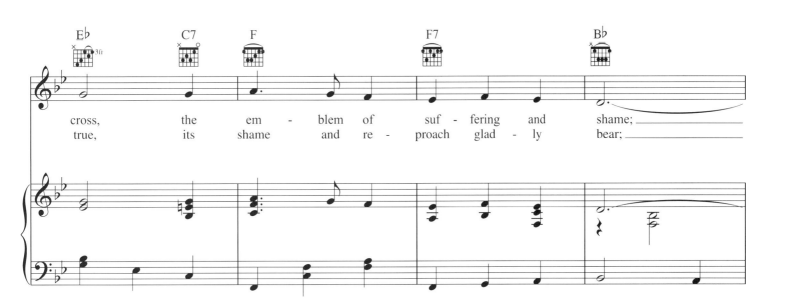

cross, the em - blem of suf - fering and shame; ____
true, its shame and re - proach glad - ly bear; ____

down; _____ I will cling to the old rug - ged

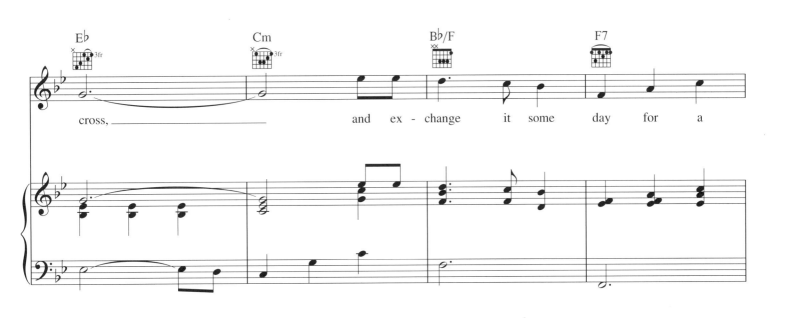

cross, _____ and ex - change it some day for a

crown. _____ To the crown. _____

THE LILY OF THE VALLEY

Words by CHARLES W. FRY
Music by WILLIAM S. HAYS

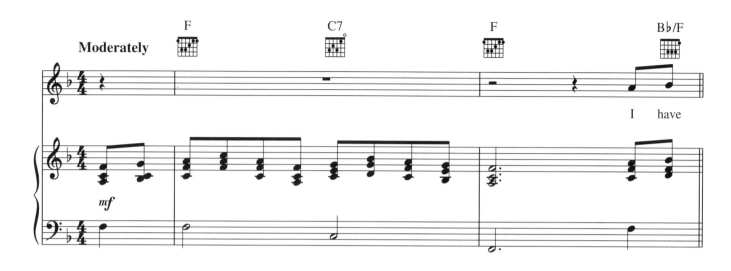

I have

found a friend in Je - sus, He's ev - 'ry - thing to me, He's the
all my grief has tak - en, and all my sor - rows borne; In temp -
nev - er, nev - er leave me, nor yet for - sake me here, While I

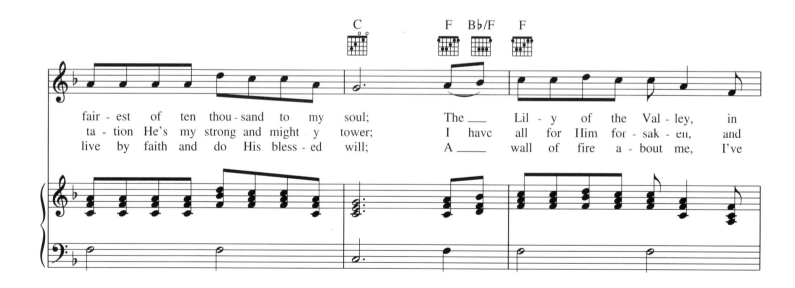

fair - est of ten thou - sand to my soul; The __ Lil - y of the Val - ley, in
ta - tion He's my strong and might - y tower; I have all for Him for - sak - en, and
live by faith and do His bless - ed will; A __ wall of fire a - bout me, I've

THE LORD'S MY SHEPHERD, I'LL NOT WANT

Words from *Scottish Psalter,* 1650
Based on Psalm 23
Music by JESSIE S. IRVINE

THE LOVE OF GOD

Words and Music by
FREDERICK M. LEHMAN

A MIGHTY FORTRESS IS OUR GOD

Words and Music by MARTIN LUTHER
Translated by FREDERICK H. HEDGE
Based on Psalm 46

With Majesty

A might-y for-tress is ___ our God, a bul-wark nev-er
we in our _ own strength_con-fide, our striv-ing would be

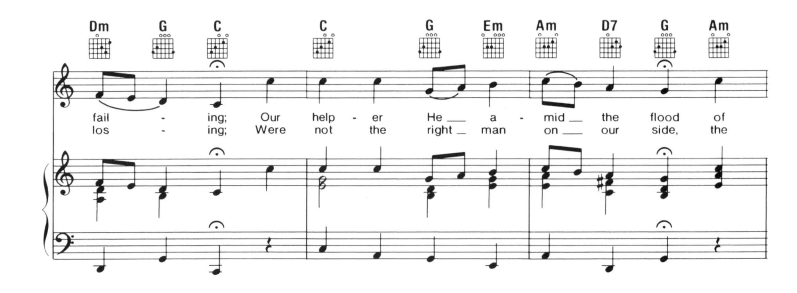

fail - ing; Our help - er He ___ a - mid ___ the flood of
los - ing; Were not the right ___ man on ___ our side, the

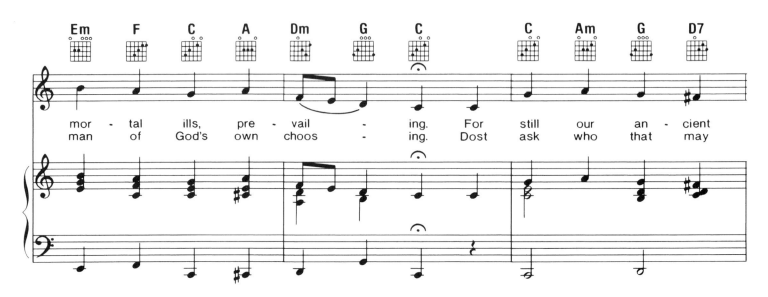

mor - tal ills, pre - vail - ing. For still our an - cient
man of God's own choos - ing. For Dost ask who that may

3. And tho this world, with devils filled,
Should threaten to undo us;
We will not fear, for God hath willed
His truth to triumph through us;
The Prince of darkness grim,
We tremble not for him;
His rage we can endure,
For lo! His doom is sure,
One little word shall fell him.

4. That word above all earthly powers,
No thanks to them abideth,
The spirit and the gifts are ours
Through Him who with us sideth;
Let goods and kindred go,
This mortal life also;
The body they may kill;
God's truth abideth still,
His kingdom is forever.

MY FAITH HAS FOUND A RESTING PLACE

Words by LIDIE H. EDMUNDS
Music by ANDRÉ GRÉTRY

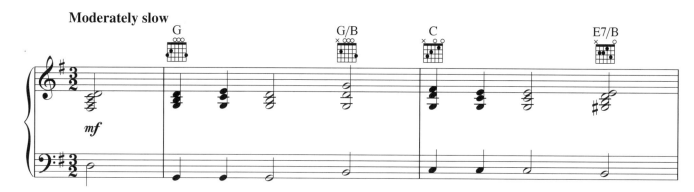

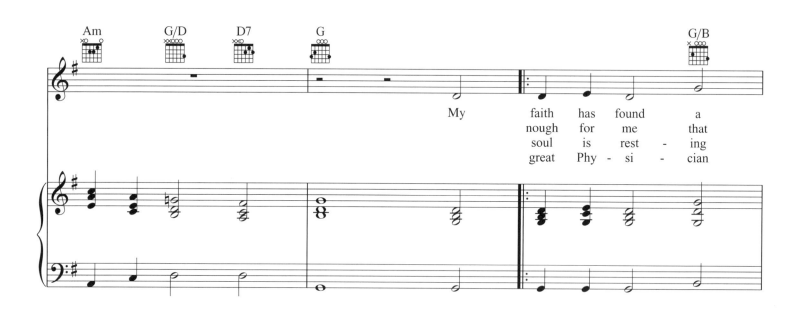

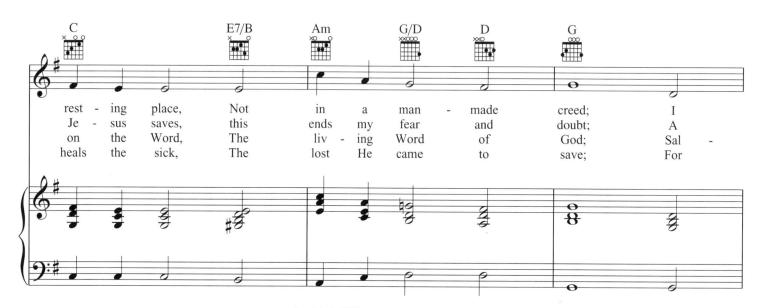

MY FAITH LOOKS UP TO THEE

Words by RAY PALMER
Music by LOWELL MASON

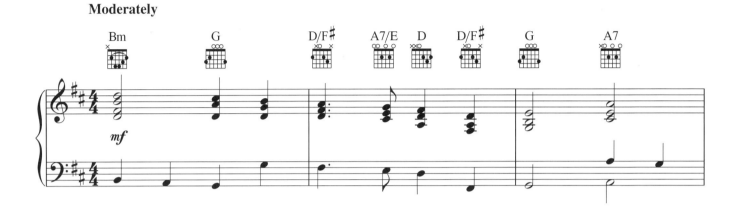

My faith looks up to Thee,
May Thy rich grace im - part
While life's dark maze I tread
When ends life's pass - ing dream,

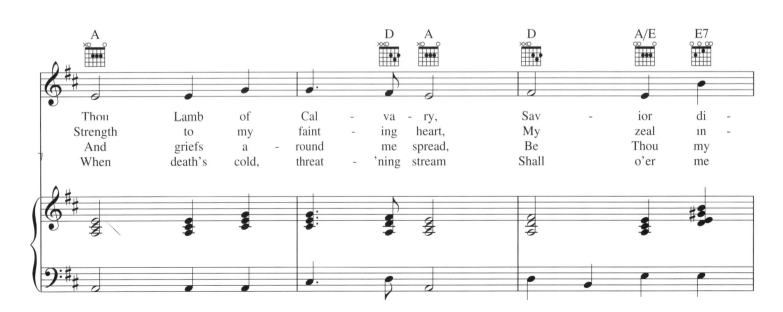

Thou Lamb of Cal - va - ry,
Strength to my faint - ing heart,
And griefs a - round me spread,
When death's cold, threat - 'ning stream

Sav - ior di -
My zeal in -
Be Thou my
Shall o'er me

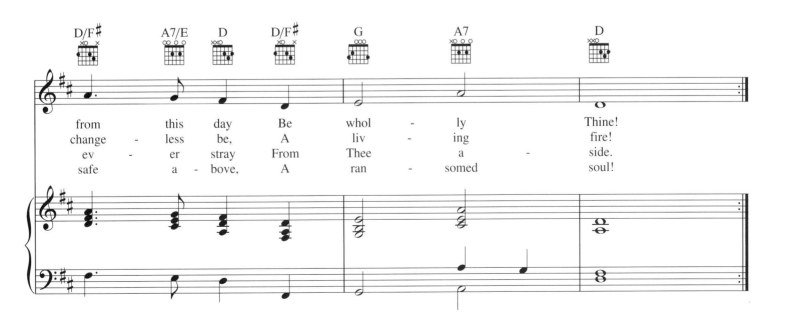

NEARER, MY GOD, TO THEE

Words by SARAH F. ADAMS
Based on Genesis 28:10-22
Music by LOWELL MASON

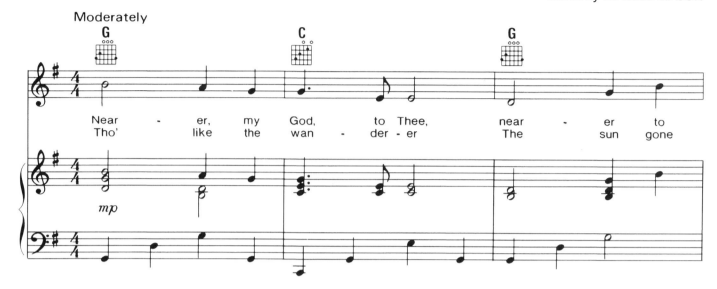

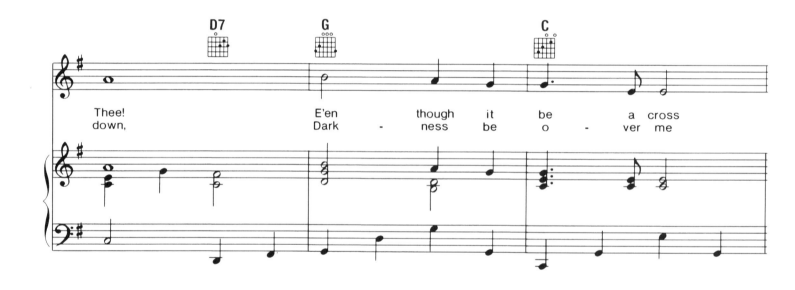

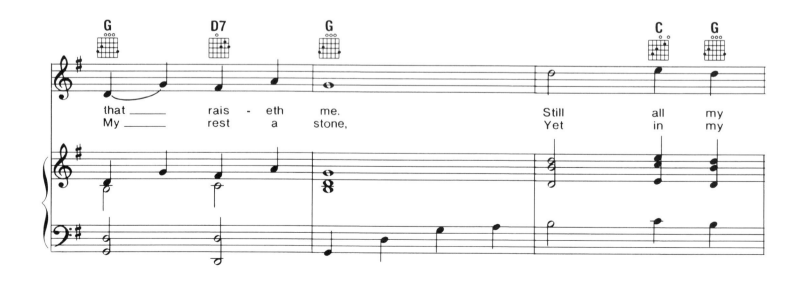

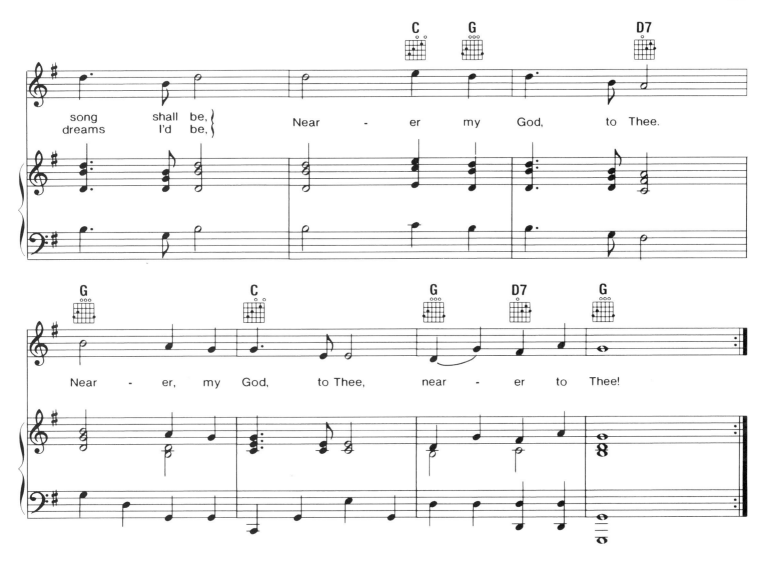

song shall be, } Near - er my God, to Thee.
dreams I'd be, }

Near - er, my God, to Thee, near - er to Thee!

3. Then with my waking tho'ts
   Bright with Thy praise,
   Out of my stony griefs
   Bethel I'll raise
   So by my woes to be,
   Nearer, my God, to Thee,
   Nearer, my God, to Thee,
   Nearer to Thee!

4. Or if on joyful wing,
   Cleaving the sky,
   Sun, moon, and stars forgot,
   Upwards I'll fly,
   Still all my song shall be,
   Nearer, my God, to Thee,
   Nearer, my God, to Thee,
   Nearer to Thee!

A NEW NAME IN GLORY

Words and Music by
C. AUSTIN MILES

Joyfully

I was once a sin-ner, but I came,
I was hum-bly kneel-ing at the cross,
In the book 'tis writ-ten, "Saved by grace."

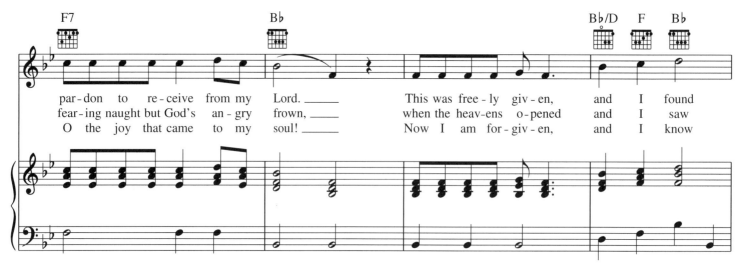

par-don to re-ceive from my Lord. _____ This was free-ly giv-en, and I found
fear-ing naught but God's an-gry frown, _____ when the heav-ens o-pened and I saw
O the joy that came to my soul! _____ Now I am for-giv-en, and I know

that He al-ways kept His word. }
that my name was writ-ten down. } There's a new name writ-ten down in glo-ry, _____ and it's
by the blood I am made whole. }

NOBODY KNOWS THE TROUBLE I'VE SEEN

African-American Spiritual

NOW THANK WE ALL OUR GOD

German Words by MARTIN RINKART
English Translation by CATHERINE WINKWORTH
Music by JOHANN CRÜGER

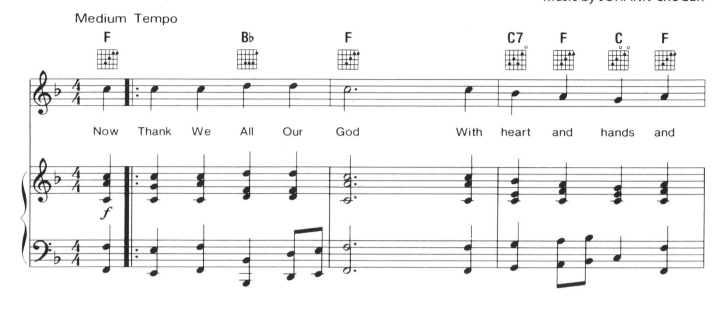

Now Thank We All Our God With heart and hands and

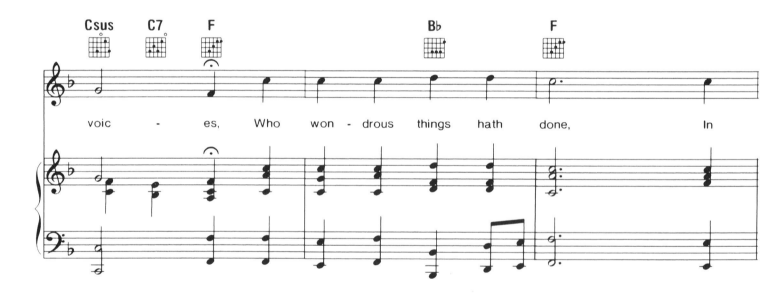

voic - es, Who won - drous things hath done, In

whom His world re - joic - es; Who, from our moth - er's arms, Hath

2. (O) may this bounteous God
Through all our life be near us,
With ever joyful hearts
And blessed peace to cheer us;
And keep us in His grace,
And guide us when perplexed,
And free us from all ills,
In this world and the next.

3. (All) praise and thanks to God
The Father now be given,
The Son and Him who reigns
With them in highest heaven;
The one eternal God,
Whom earth and heav'n adore;
For thus it was, is now,
And shall be evermore.

NOW THE DAY IS OVER

Words by SABINE BARING-GOULD
Music by JOSEPH BARNBY

ONLY BELIEVE

Words and Music by
PAUL RADER

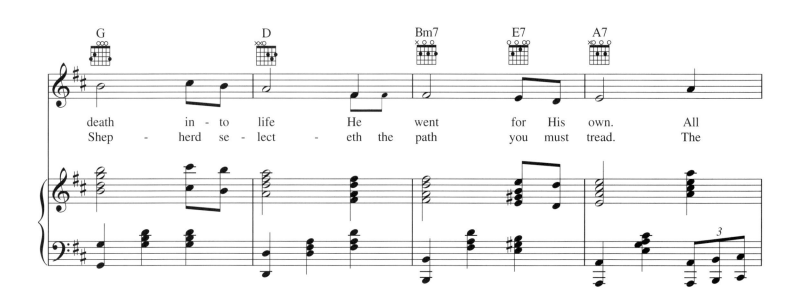

PRAISE HIM! PRAISE HIM!

Words by FANNY J. CROSBY
Music by CHESTER G. ALLEN

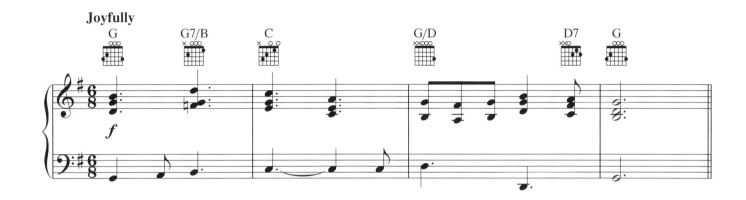

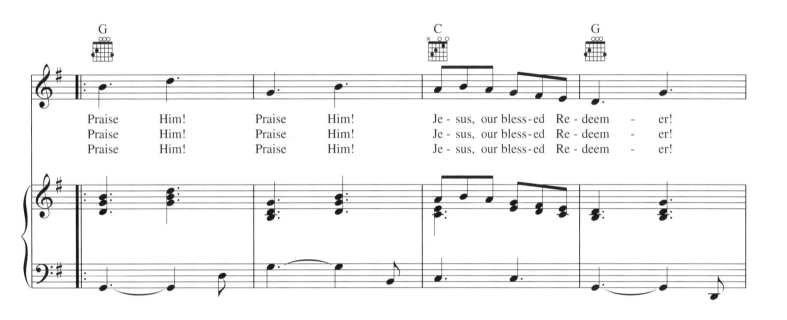

Praise Him! Praise Him! Je - sus, our bless-ed Re - deem - er!
Praise Him! Praise Him! Je - sus, our bless-ed Re - deem - er!
Praise Him! Praise Him! Je - sus, our bless-ed Re - deem - er!

Sing, O Earth, His won - der - ful love pro - claim!
For our sins He suf - fered and bled and died.
Heav'n - ly por - tals loud with ho - san - nas ring!

Hail Him, Hail Him, high-est arch-an-gels in glo-ry;
He, our Rock, our hope of e-ter-nal sal-va-tion;
Je-sus, Sav-ior, reign-eth for-ev-er and ev-er;

Strength and hon-or give to His ho-ly name!
Hail Him! Hail Him! Je-sus, the cru-ci-fied.
Crown Him! Crown Him! Proph-et and Priest and King!

Like a shep-herd, Je-sus will guard His chil-dren;
Sound His prais-es, Je-sus who bore our sor-rows;
Christ is com-ing, o-ver the world vic-to-rious;

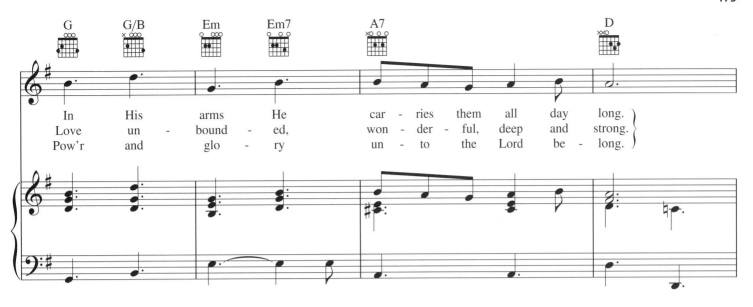

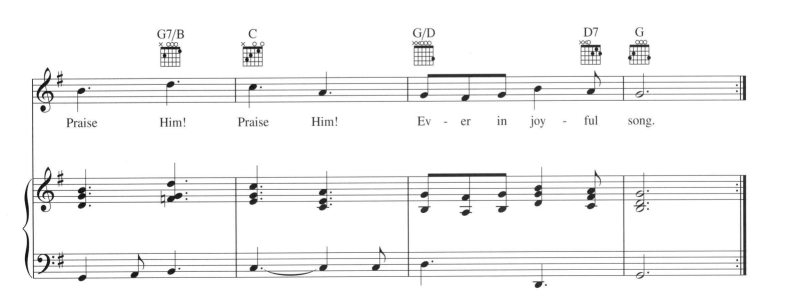

ONWARD, CHRISTIAN SOLDIERS

Words by SABINE BARING-GOULD
Music by ARTHUR S. SULLIVAN

PRAISE TO THE LORD,
THE ALMIGHTY

Words by JOACHIM NEANDER
Translated by CATHERINE WINKWORTH
Music from *Erneuerten Gesangbuch*

ROCK OF AGES

Words by AUGUSTUS M. TOPLADY
Music by THOMAS HASTINGS

RING THE BELLS OF HEAVEN

Words by WILLIAM O. CUSHING
Music by GEORGE F. ROOT

Ring the bells of heav - en! There is joy to - day,
Ring the bells of heav - en! There is joy to - day,
Ring the bells of heav - en! Spread the feast to - day!

For a soul, re - turn - ing from the wild!
For the wan - der - er now is rec - on - ciled;
An - gels swell the glad tri - um - phant strain!

See, the Fa - ther meets him out up - on the way,
Yes, a soul is res - cued from his sin - ful way,
Tell the joy - ful tid - ings, Bear it far a - way!

SAVIOR, LIKE A SHEPHERD LEAD US

Words from *Hymns For The Young*
Attributed to DOROTHY A. THRUPP
Music by WILLIAM B. BRADBURY

Quietly

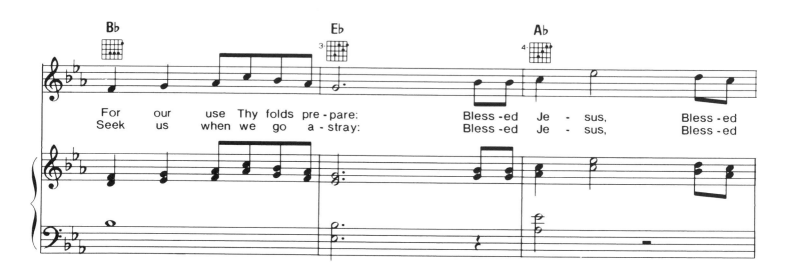

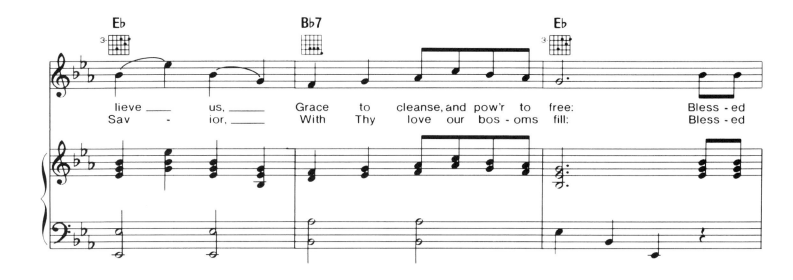

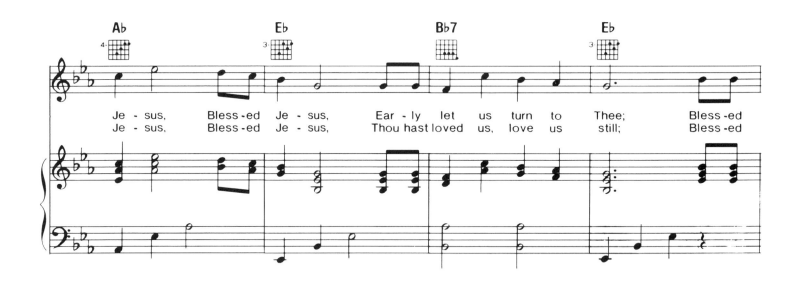

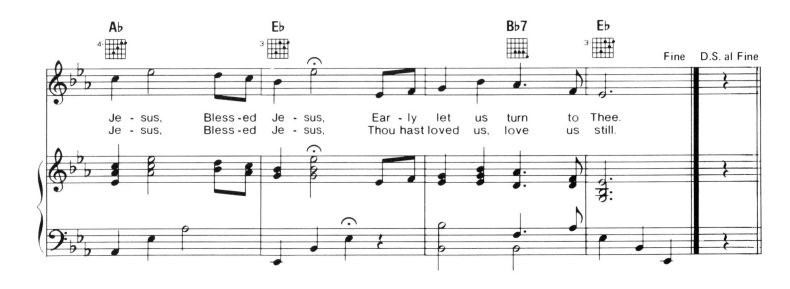

STAND UP AND BLESS THE LORD

Words and Music by JAMES MONTGOMERY
Music by CHARLES LOCKHART

SHALL WE GATHER AT THE RIVER?

Words and Music by
ROBERT LOWRY

Shall we gath-er at the riv - er, Where bright an-gel feet have

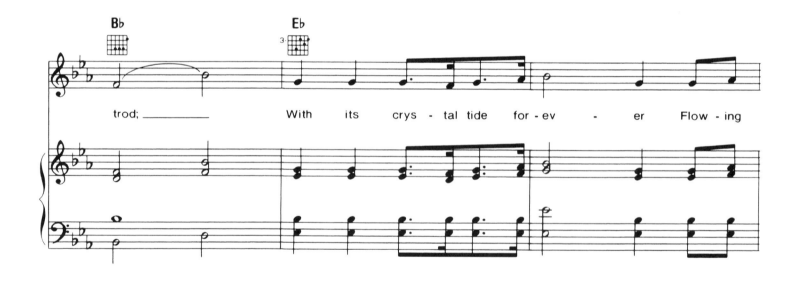

trod; _____ With its crys - tal tide for-ev - er Flow-ing

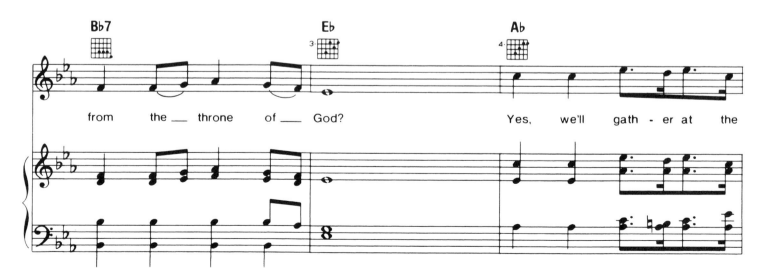

from the ___ throne of ___ God? Yes, we'll gath-er at the

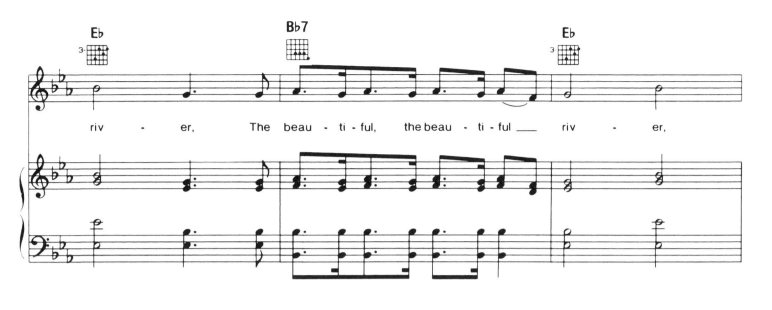

river, The beau - ti - ful, the beau - ti - ful ___ riv - er,

Gath - er with the saints at the riv - er, That flows from the throne of __ God.

2. On the margin of the river,
   Washing up its silver spray,
   We shall walk and worship ever
   All the happy, golden day.

3. On the bosom of the river,
   Where the Saviour King we own,
   We shall meet and sorrow never
   'Neath the glory of the throne.

4. Ere we reach the shining river,
   Lay we ev'ry burden down:
   Grace our spirits will deliver,
   And provide a robe and crown.

5. Soon we'll reach the shining river,
   Soon our pilgrimage will cease;
   Soon our happy hearts will quiver
   With the melody of peace.

STAND UP, STAND UP FOR JESUS

Words by GEORGE DUFFIELD, JR.
Music by GEORGE J. WEBB

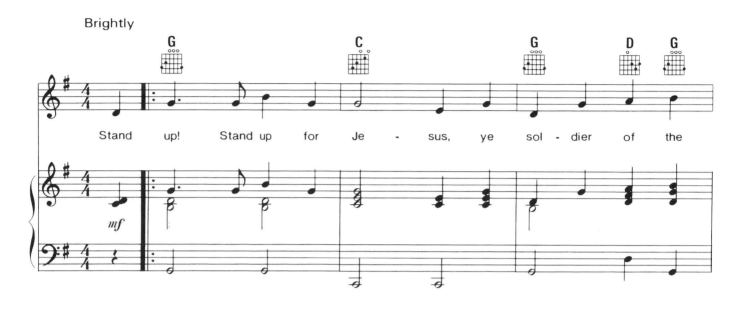

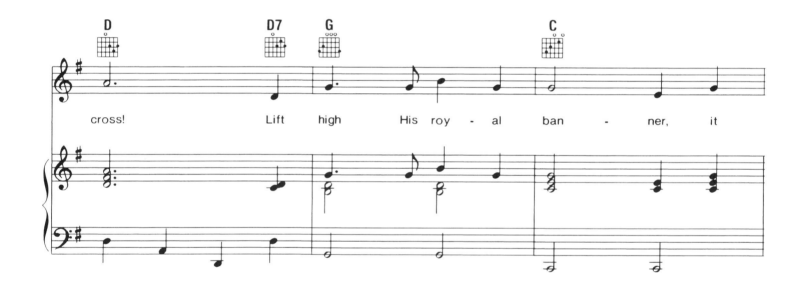

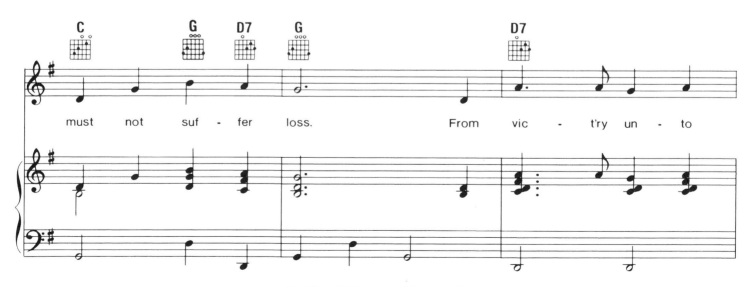

vic - t'ry His ar - my shall He lead, _____ Till ev - 'ry foe is

van - quished and Christ is Lord in - deed. Stand ly.

2. Stand up, stand up for Jesus,
The strife will not be long;
This day the noise of battle,
The next, the victor's song;
To him the overcometh,
A crown of life shall be;
He with the King of glory
Shall reign eternally.

STANDING ON THE PROMISES

Words and Music by
R. KELSO CARTER

1. Stand-ing on the prom-is-es of
2.-4. *(See additional verses)*

Christ my King, Thru e-ter-nal a-ges let His prais-es ring;

Glo-ry in the high-est, I will shout and sing, Stand-ing on the prom-is-es of

Additional Verses

2. Standing on the promises that cannot fail,
When the howling storms of doubt and fear assail,
By the living word of God I shall prevail,
Standing on the promises of God.
Refrain

3. Standing on the promises of Christ the Lord,
Bound to Him eternally by love's strong cord,
Overcoming daily with the Spirit's sword,
Standing on the promises of God.
Refrain

4. Standing on the promises I cannot fall,
Listening ev'ry moment to the Spirit's call,
Resting in my Savior as my all in all,
Standing on the promises of God.
Refrain

STEAL AWAY
(Steal Away to Jesus)

Traditional Spiritual

TELL ME THE STORIES OF JESUS

Words by WILLIAM H. PARKER
Music by FREDERIC A. CHALLINOR

TAKE MY LIFE AND LET IT BE

Words by FRANCES R. HAVERGAL
Music by HENRY A. CÉSAR MALAN

THERE IS A FOUNTAIN

Words by WILLIAM COWPER
Traditional American Melody
Arranged by LOWELL MASON

Additional Verses

2. The dying thief rejoiced to see
   That fountain in his day;
   And there may I, though vile as he,
   Wash all my sins away:...

3. Dear dying Lamb, Thy precious blood
   Shall never lose its power,
   Till all the ransomed Church of God
   Be saved, to sin no more:...

4. E'er since by faith, I saw the stream
   Thy flowing wounds supply,
   Redeeming love has been my theme,
   And shall be till I die:...

5. Then in a nobler, sweeter song,
   I'll sing Thy power to save,
   When this poor lisping, stamm'ring tongue
   Lies silent in the grave. Amen.

THINE IS THE GLORY

Words by EDMOND LOUIS BUDRY
Music by GEORGE FRIDERIC HANDEL

Victoriously

Thine is the glo - ry, ris - en, __ con - quering Son.
Lo! Je - sus meets us, ris - en __ from the tomb.
No more we doubt Thee, glo - rious __ Prince of life!

End - less __ is the vic - t'ry Thou o'er death hast won.
Lov - ing - ly He greets us, scat - ters fear and gloom.
Life __ is __ nought with - out Thee; aid us in our strife.

THIS LITTLE LIGHT OF MINE

African-American Spiritual

TURN YOUR EYES UPON JESUS

Words and Music by
HELEN H. LEMMEL

TRUST AND OBEY

Words by JOHN H. SAMMIS
Music by DANIEL B. TOWNER

WAYFARING STRANGER

Southern American Folk Hymn

WERE YOU THERE?

Traditional Spiritual

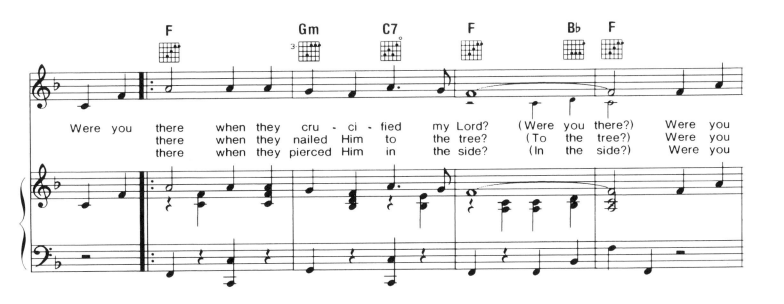

Were you there when they cru-ci-fied my Lord? (Were you there?) Were you
there when they nailed Him to the tree? (To the tree?) Were you
there when they pierced Him in the side? (In the side?) Were you

there when they cru-ci-fied my Lord? _____ Oh, _____
there when they nailed Him to the tree? _____ Oh, _____
there when they pierced Him in the side? _____ Oh, _____

WE GATHER TOGETHER

Words from *Nederlandtsch Gedenckclanck*
Netherlands Folk Melody

WE WOULD SEE JESUS

Words by ANNA B. WARNER
Music by FRANKLIN E. BELDEN

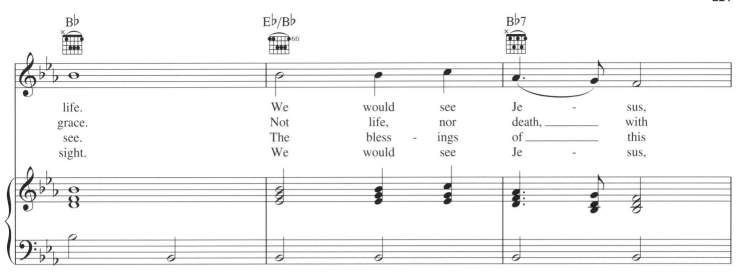

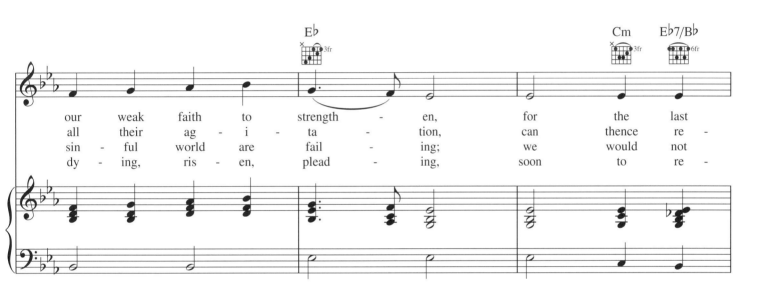

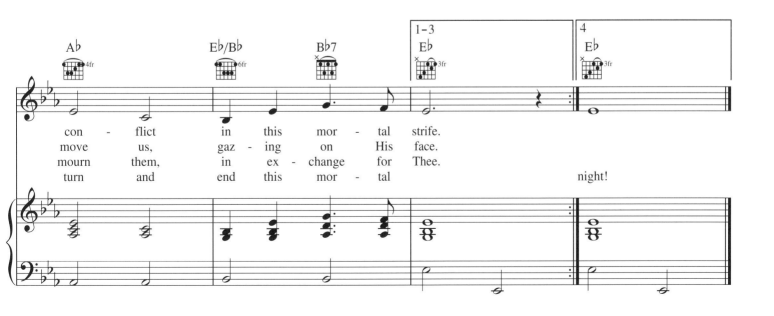

WE'RE MARCHING TO ZION

Words by ISAAC WATTS and ROBERT LOWRY
Music by ROBERT LOWRY

Additional Verses

2. Let those refuse to sing
    Who never knew our God;
    But children of the heav'nly King,
    But children of the heav'nly King,
    May speak their joys abroad,
    May speak their joys abroad.
    Refrain

3. The hill of Zion yields
    A thousand sacred sweets,
    Before we reach the heav'nly fields,
    Before we reach the heav'nly fields,
    Or walk the golden streets,
    Or walk the golden streets.
    Refrain

4. Then let our songs abound,
    And ev'ry tear be dry;
    We're marching thru Immanuel's ground,
    We're marching thru Immanuel's ground,
    To fairer worlds on high,
    To fairer worlds on high.
    Refrain

WHAT A FRIEND WE HAVE IN JESUS

Words by JOSEPH M. SCRIVEN
Music by CHARLES C. CONVERSE

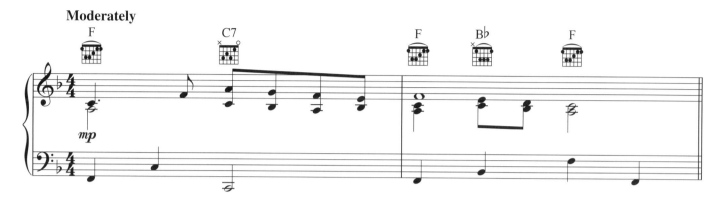

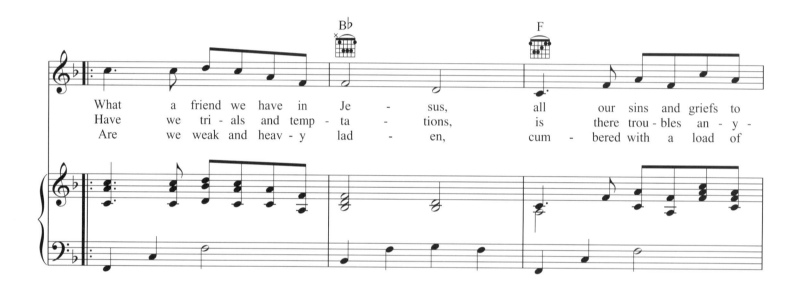

What a friend we have in Je - sus, all our sins and griefs to
Have we tri - als and temp - ta - tions, is there trou - bles an - y -
Are we weak and heav - y lad - en, cum - bered with a load of

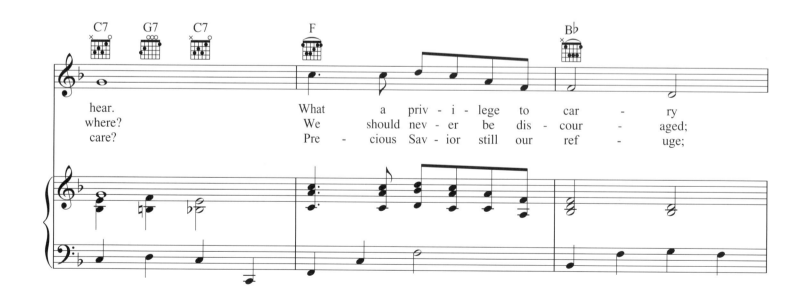

hear. What a priv - i - lege to car - ry
where? We should nev - er be dis - cour - aged;
care? Pre - cious Sav - ior still our ref - uge;

225

WHEN I SURVEY THE WONDROUS CROSS

Words by ISAAC WATTS
Music arranged by LOWELL MASON
Based on Plainsong

Moderately

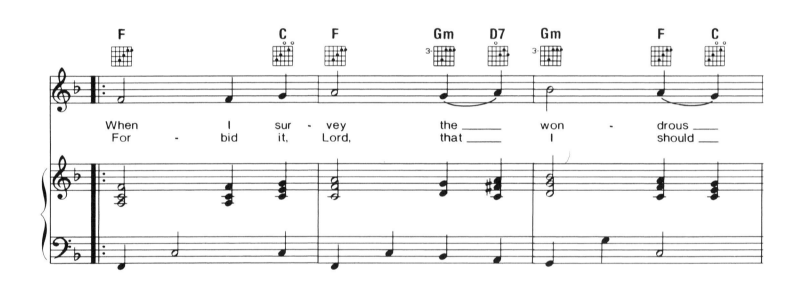

When I sur-vey the won - drous cross
For - bid it, Lord, that I should

cross On which the Prince of
boast Save in the death of

3. See, from His head, His hands, His feet,
   Sorrow and love flow mingled down
   Did e'er such love and sorrow meet
   Or thorns compose so rich a crown.

4. Were the whole realm of nature mine,
   That were a present far too small.
   Love so amazing so divine,
   Demands my soul, my life, my all.

WHEN THE SAINTS GO MARCHING IN

Words by KATHERINE E. PURVIS
Music by JAMES M. BLACK

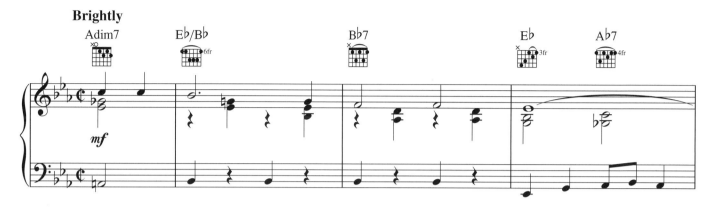

Oh, when the saints _____ go march - ing
sun _____ re - fuse to
crown _____ Him Lord of
gath - er 'round the

in, _____ Oh, when the saints go march - ing
shine, _____ Oh, when the sun re - fuse to
all, _____ Oh, when they crown Him Lord of
throne, _____ Oh, when they gath - er 'round the

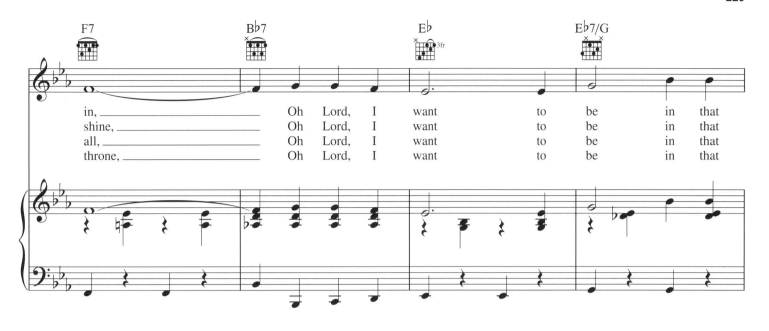

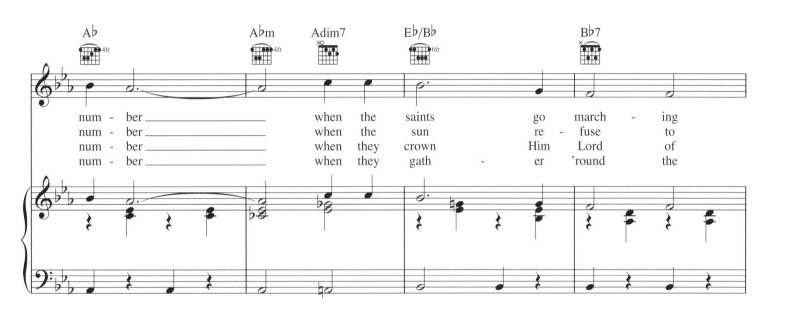

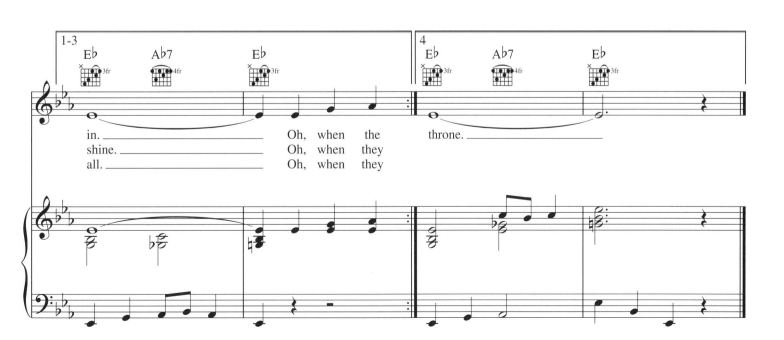

WHISPERING HOPE

Words and Music by
ALICE HAWTHORNE

WHITER THAN SNOW

Words by JAMES L. NICHOLSON
Music by WILLIAM G. FISCHER

1. Lord Je - sus, I long to be per - fect - ly whole; I

2.-4. *(See additional verses)*

want Thee for - ev - er to live in my soul, Break

down ev - ery i - dol, cast out ev - 'ry foe; Now

Additional Verses

2. Lord Jesus, look down from Thy throne in the skies,
   And help me to make a complete sacrifice;
   I give up myself, and whatever I know,
   Now wash me and I shall be whiter than snow.
   Refrain

3. Lord Jesus, for this I most humbly entreat,
   I wait, blessed Lord, at Thy crucified feet;
   By faith, for my cleansing I see Thy blood flow,
   Now wash me and I shall be whiter than snow.
   Refrain

4. Lord Jesus, Thou seeest I patiently wait,
   Come now, and within me a new heart create;
   To those who have sought Thee, Thou never saidst "No,"
   Now wash me and I shall be whiter than snow.
   Refrain

WONDROUS LOVE

Southern American Folk Hymn

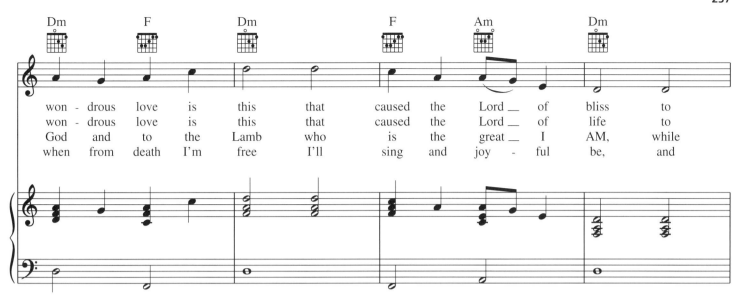

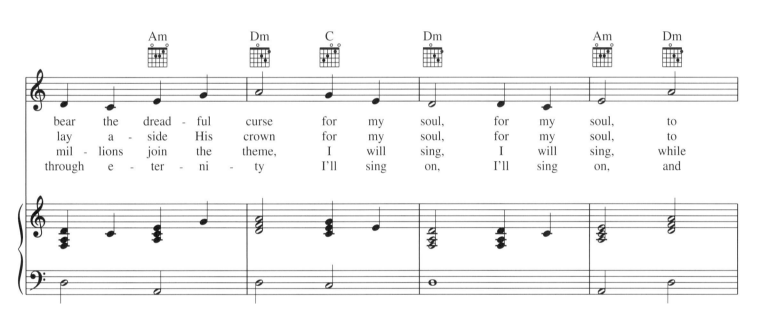

WORK, FOR THE NIGHT IS COMING

Words by ANNIE L. COGHILL
Music by LOWELL MASON

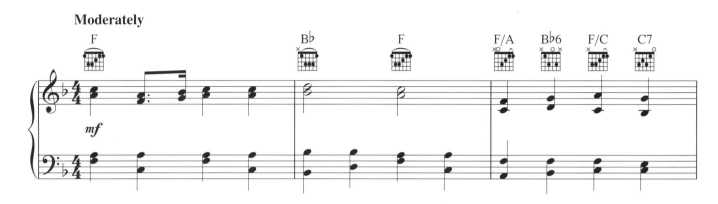

Work, for the night is com - ing,
Work, for the night is com - ing,
Work, for the night is com - ing,

work through the morn - ing hours.
work through the sun - ny noon.
un - der the sun - set skies.

Work while the dew is
Fill bright - est hours with
While their bright tints are

Play the best songs from the Roaring '20s to today! Each collection features dozens of the most memorable songs of each decade, or in your favorite musical style, arranged in piano/vocal/guitar format.

THE 1920s
Over 100 songs that shaped the decade: Ain't We Got Fun? • Basin Street Blues • Bye Bye Blackbird • Can't Help Lovin' Dat Man • I Wanna Be Loved by You • Makin' Whoopee • Ol' Man River • Puttin' On the Ritz • Toot, Toot, Tootsie • Yes Sir, That's My Baby • and more.
00311200 ....$24.95

THE 1930s
97 essential songs from the 1930s: April in Paris • Body and Soul • Cheek to Cheek • Falling in Love with Love • Georgia on My Mind • Heart and Soul • I'll Be Seeing You • The Lady Is a Tramp • Mood Indigo • My Funny Valentine • You Are My Sunshine • and more.
00311193 ....$24.95

THE 1940s
An amazing collection of over 100 songs from the '40s: Boogie Woogie Bugle Boy • Don't Get Around Much Anymore • Have I Told You Lately That I Love You • I'll Remember April • Route 66 • Sentimental Journey • Take the "A" Train • You'd Be So Nice to Come Home To • and more.
00311192 ....$24.95

THE 1950s
Over 100 pivotal songs from the 1950s, including: All Shook Up • Bye Bye Love • Chantilly Lace • Fever • Great Balls of Fire • Kansas City • Love and Marriage • Mister Sandman • Rock Around the Clock • Sixteen Tons • Tennessee Waltz • Wonderful! Wonderful! • and more.
00311191 ....$24.95

THE 1960s
104 '60s essentials, including: Baby Love • California Girls • Dancing in the Street • Hey Jude • I Heard It Through the Grapevine • Respect • Stand by Me • Twist and Shout • Will You Love Me Tomorrow • Yesterday • You Keep Me Hangin' On • and more.
00311190 ....$24.95

THE 1970s
Over 80 of the best songs from the '70s: American Pie • Band on the Run • Come Sail Away • Dust in the Wind • I Feel the Earth Move • Let It Be • Morning Has Broken • Smoke on the Water • Take a Chance on Me • The Way We Were • You're So Vain • and more.
00311189 ....$24.95

THE 1980s
Over 70 classics from the age of power pop and hair metal: Against All Odds • Call Me • Ebony and Ivory • The Heat Is On • Jump • Manic Monday • Sister Christian • Time After Time • Up Where We Belong • What's Love Got to Do with It • and more.
00311188 ....$24.95

Complete contents listings are available online at 🏠

THE 1990s
68 songs featuring country-crossover, swing revival, the birth of grunge, and more: Change the World • Fields of Gold • Ironic • Livin' La Vida Loca • More Than Words • Smells like Teen Spirit • Walking in Memphis • Zoot Suit Riot • and more.
00311187 ....$24.95

THE 2000s
59 of the best songs that brought in the new millennium: Accidentally in Love • Beautiful • Don't Know Why • Get the Party Started • Hey Ya! • I Hope You Dance • 1985 • This Love • A Thousand Miles • Wherever You Will Go • Who Let the Dogs Out • You Raise Me Up • and more.
00311186 ....$24.95

ACOUSTIC ROCK
Over 70 songs, including: About a Girl • Barely Breathing • Blowin' in the Wind • Fast Car • Landslide • Turn! Turn! Turn! (To Everything There Is a Season) • Walk on the Wild Side • and more.
00311747 ....$24.95

THE BEATLES
Over 90 of the finest from this extraordinary band: All My Loving • Back in the U.S.S.R. • Blackbird • Come Together • Get Back • Help! • Hey Jude • If I Fell • Let It Be • Michelle • Penny Lane • Something • Twist and Shout • Yesterday • more!
00311389 ....$24.95

BROADWAY
Over 90 songs of the stage: Any Dream Will Do • Blue Skies • Cabaret • Don't Cry for Me, Argentina • Edelweiss • Hello, Dolly! • I'll Be Seeing You • Memory • The Music of the Night • Oklahoma • Summer Nights • There's No Business Like Show Business • Tomorrow • more.
00311222 ....$24.95

CHILDREN'S SONGS
Over 110 songs, including: Bob the Builder "Intro Theme Song" • "C" Is for Cookie • Eensy Weensy Spider • I'm Popeye the Sailor Man • The Muppet Show Theme • Old MacDonald • Sesame Street Theme • and more.
00311823 ....$24.99

CHRISTMAS
Over 100 essential holiday favorites: Blue Christmas • The Christmas Song • Deck the Hall • Frosty the Snow Man • Joy to the World • Merry Christmas, Darling • Rudolph the Red-Nosed Reindeer • Silver Bells • and more!
00311241 ....$24.95

COUNTRY
96 essential country standards, including: Achy Breaky Heart • Crazy • The Devil Went down to Georgia • Elvira • Friends in Low Places • God Bless the U.S.A. • Here You Come Again • Lucille • Redneck Woman • Tennessee Waltz • and more.
00311296 ....$24.95

JAZZ STANDARDS
99 jazz classics no music library should be without: Autumn in New York • Body and Soul • Don't Get Around Much Anymore • Easy to Love (You'd Be So Easy to Love) • I've Got You Under My Skin • The Lady Is a Tramp • Mona Lisa • Satin Doll • Stardust • Witchcraft • and more.
00311226 ....$24.95

LOVE SONGS
Over 80 romantic hits: Can You Feel the Love Tonight • Endless Love • From This Moment On • Have I Told You Lately • I Just Called to Say I Love You • Love Will Keep Us Together • My Heart Will Go On • Wonderful Tonight • You Are So Beautiful • more.
00311235 ....$24.95

LOVE STANDARDS
100 romantic standards: Dream a Little Dream of Me • The Glory of Love • I Left My Heart in San Francisco • I've Got My Love to Keep Me Warm • The Look of Love • A Time for Us • You Are the Sunshine of My Life • and more.
00311256 ....$24.95

MOVIE SONGS
94 of the most popular silver screen songs: Alfie • Beauty and the Beast • Chariots of Fire • Footloose • I Will Remember You • Jailhouse Rock • Moon River • People • Somewhere Out There • Summer Nights • Unchained Melody • and more.
00311236 ....$24.95

ROCK
Over 80 essential rock classics: Black Magic Woman • Day Tripper • Free Bird • A Groovy Kind of Love • I Shot the Sheriff • The Joker • My Sharona • Oh, Pretty Woman • Proud Mary • Rocket Man • Roxanne • Takin' Care of Business • A Whiter Shade of Pale • Wild Thing • more!
00311390 ....$24.95

TV SONGS
Over 100 terrific tube tunes, including: The Addams Family Theme • Bonanza • The Brady Bunch • Desperate Housewives Main Title • I Love Lucy • Law and Order • Linus and Lucy • Sesame Street Theme • Theme from the Simpsons • Theme from the X-Files • and more!
00311223 ....$24.95

WEDDING
83 songs of love and devotion: All I Ask of You • Canon in D • Don't Know Much • Here, There and Everywhere • Love Me Tender • My Heart Will Go On • Somewhere Out There • Wedding March • You Raise Me Up • and more.
00311309 ....$24.95

FOR MORE INFORMATION, SEE YOUR LOCAL MUSIC DEALER, OR WRITE TO:

HAL•LEONARD® CORPORATION
7777 W. BLUEMOUND RD. P.O. BOX 13819 MILWAUKEE, WI 53213

Prices, contents and availability subject to change without notice.

0209